Human Emotions

and Excitements

Human Emotions and Excitements

Internal Evil in Disguise

Rokneddin Darvish, Ph. D

ISBN: 1533612773
ISBN 13: 9781533612779

Dedicated to:
My wife Susan and my sons Babak and Siamak
For their inspirations and support

Autobiography

Rokneddin Darvish, Ph. D is a licensed behavior specialist in the State of Utah at present. He has received his BA in English language and literature and social sciences from the University of Tehran, MS in sociology and psychology from the Texas A&I University, Ph. D in sociology, social organization and disorganization from North Texas State University (now University of North Texas), and a (Post Doctorate) Certification Degree in School Psychology from University of Utah. His work history includes: working with Juvenile Delinquents at State School in Texas for 3 years, Inmates at Utah State Prison for 5 years and provided psychological and behavioral services for individuals with developmental disabilities, autism and mental illness for 21 years at Utah State Developmental Center, and the Utah State Prison in Utah. Population he served includes Individuals with developmental disability, mental illness and criminal behaviors as well as students with behavior problems in schools and older population in care centers.

Dr. Darvish worked in different capacities including Behavior Specialist/Analyst Consultant, Program Support Supervisor, Caseworker II, Dorm Director, Dean of Faculty, President and Executive Director of University. In addition he provided behavioral services for total of 26 years as a Ph. D behavior specialist/analyst and BC III (Behavior consultant III), working with individuals with Autism, developmental disabilities and individuals with mental illness in different communities in Utah. He retired from the State of Utah on July, 2010.

Dr. Darvish presented many topics in the area of developmental disability, mental illness and behavior analysis at various professional conferences and completed several research projects and coauthored several articles published in the behavior analytic and scientific journals in the United States of America. He is also author of a book entitled "Consciousness, Mental system and mental self" (under publication).

Preface

In this second book I have tried to provide a psychological approach reflecting Rumi's philosophy and ideas regarding the distinction between human positive excitements and emotions as characteristics of universal consciousness which is the source of joy, creativity and tranquility, and human negative excitements, emotions, and deficiencies as the main traits of human mental system as an internal hell and mental self as an agent of evil, a source of human pains, depression, anxiety and sufferings. Rumi's poems and messages represent human conversion from an immature mental self with polluted and impure consciousness and distorted thought, emotions, and excitements, to the real, objective self or pure consciousness. Some recommendations are made about the methods of conversion such as patience, silence, relaxation, and acceptance of the events and incidents of this moment without any reaction, resistance and judgement. The nature of acceptance is total acceptance without fighting against the event or incident of this moment, and consciously surrendering to the universal consciousness. What Rumi tried to present to all human beings is the art of living and loving.

According to Rumi, we should concentrate on our positive emotions and love and experience the unconditional love instead of conditional and selfish love. We can only really become aware of another person's essence by falling in love with that person. If there is a real unconditional love, then, it is the universal consciousness trapped in one person's body falling in love with itself as a consciousness in another person's body. In this case the physical sexual attraction is only a small part of a greater spiritual attraction of consciousness in two separate bodies which is an eternal love. But when a mental self falls in love with another mental self it is not real love but only a short lived passion and sexual physical attraction. Along with love of life, Rumi emphasizes on the recognition and awareness of human being of universal consciousness which resides within us and constantly working through us and helps us to free ourselves of the dark prison of mental system by deactivating and finally dissolving our mental self or internal evil. We can escape all these pain and sufferings by being patient and unconditionally accepting our situation.

All our negative emotions, excitements, pains and suffering comes from our pain addicting mental self as an internal evil and, the biased mental system with limited capacity as an internal hell. Mental self is unidimensional and works only through duality and comparing and contrasting two opposites or complementary phenomena. Mental self only concentrates on negative emotions and excitements as well as living in the psychological time of the past and becomes depressed as related to the negative events of the past and becomes anxious and worried as related to the probable events of the future. Thus, two major emotional and psychological problems of human beings relate to the mental system and mental self by emphasizing on the psychological time of the past or the present which are distorted mental concepts and do not have any real basis in reality. Escaping from the real time of the present or this moment would not let human to concentrate on the existing life of the present time and would not let be able to enjoy life to the maximum possible level.

The main topics of discussion include: Human excitements and emotions created by mental self within the mental system as the source of our pain and sufferings; Externalized human emotions or excessive and exaggerated emotions that create our explosive and aggressive behaviors; Internalized human emotions which are the source of our sadness and depression with the exception of love, sympathy, empathy, nurturing and caring that are both positive emotions but can be internalized or externalized based on different situations.

Other characteristics of emotions or excitements are discussed. Prevention and intervention strategies to cope with negative emotions and excitements are also reviewed.

Jalal-e-din Mohammad Molavi Rumi was born in 1207 BC at Balkh in the north-eastern provinces of Persia (Present day Afghanistan) to a Persian speaking family. Rumi worked as a professor in the famous Madrasah at Konya at the age of Twenty-four years. He was highly influenced by Shams-e-Tabrizi, a masterpiece of wisdom. He died in 1273 at Konya (Present day Turkey). Major works completed by Rumi are: 1. Divan-e-Shams-e-Tabrizi (Divan-e-Kabir), 2. Masnavi-e- Ma'navi the best known work of Rumi, and he himself defined his work as a work of the destruction of the worldly for the sake of embracing the Divine.-, and 3. Fihe-Ma-Fih, a collection of mystical sayings (Iran Chamber Society). Rumi's ideas, poems and scholarly works have been translated into several languages and positively affected many people across the world.

Acnowledgements

I wish to acknowledge the major contributions of Mr. Parviz Shahbazi who dedicated his life and productive time trying to introduce Rumi's Poems, works, Philosophy of life and loving, and many other Persian poets, philosophers, and mystics through a TV program called "The Treasure of Presence" and his deep analysis of the selected poems of Rumi and introduction of other scholars who have analyzed Rumi's poems. Mr. Shahbazi's interpretation of Rumi's poems had impressed me. His encouragement for Persian language speaking individuals to translate Rumi's work to other languages and to introduce them to the world was also a major motivating factor.

I have reflected human excitements and emotions that could have two opposite functions. (1) positive function for emotions as sources of joy and tranquility and (2) negative function for emotions as the sources of sadness in human life. I wrote this book in English language to introduce Rumi's ideas to the English language speaking people, utilizing a psychological and sociological approach. Rumi's works has been translated into many languages by many scholars, but my work is an analysis of Rumi's works from a psychological and sociological point of view. There are hundreds of other Persian poets, philosophers that need to be introduced to the World and I hope other people could engage in this type of scholarly endeavor.

My main acknowledgement is to the Rumi himself for his dedication to vitalize, awaken and transcend human to the highest level of spiritual joy and enlightenment through his works, poems and ideas containing his message of love that speaks directly to the heart of anyone who try to be in contact with. Familiarity and understanding of Rumi's philosophy of life and love, gives anyone a sense of inspiration and self-appreciation to know that all human have the same universal consciousness within them and to consider themselves as precious beings. Knowing that consciousness is the real essence of all humans and resides within all forms also gives a real meaning to the objective unity among all human beings and the universe.

Rumi's emphasize on the awareness and recognition of our internal consciousness that is an extension of the universal consciousness and a source of joy, tranquility and creativity as opposed to our mental system and mental self that is a source of all human evil including our miseries, negative thoughts, beliefs, opinions, customs, rites, excitements and emotions is highly awakening. It is our mental system and mental self that is causing all our physical and emotional pains and suffering. Rumi uses many stories and religious and historical events to help people to remember the stories, but his real intension is to teach the meanings behind the stories, symbols, metaphors and similes.

Table Of Content

Figures

I

Human Emotions and Excitements

"Look at love. How it tangles with one fallen in love. Look at spirit, how it fuses with earth giving it new life. Why are you so busy with this or that or good or bad, Pay attention to how things blend, Why talk about all the known and the unknown. See how the unknown merges into the known. Why think separately of this life and the next. When one is born from the last look at your heart and tongue one feels but deaf and dumb the other speaks in words and signs. Look at water and fire earth and wind enemies and friends all at once. The wolf and the lamb, the lion and the dear, far away and yet together look at the unity of this spring and winter manifested in the equinox. You too must mingle my friends since the earth and the sky are mingled just for you and me. Be like sugarcane sweet yet silent don't get mixed up with bitter words. My beloved grows right out of my own heart. How much more union can there be (Rumi) Translated by Nader Khalili).

Emotions or excitements are the driving force for our actions or behaviors. The word emotion comes from the Latin word for movement, so emotion moves and guides into action. Thus our behaviors are partly motivated by our emotions. Emotion like thought is a matter of evaluating information that we receive from our senses by emotionally responding to both internal and external stimuli. Emotions and/or excitements like thought and beliefs are part of our mental system where, our mental self originates, develops and operates. Emotion similar to thinking is also considered a sign of existence or "to be." Rumi put much emphasize on both "to be" and "to become." As the signs of existence and evolution of consciousness and love as the motivating force and positive emotion that unites us with the universal consciousness.

Gide, French intellectual once said, "I feel, therefore I am." A second statement was made by Descartes (1596-1650) stated that "I think, therefore I am" confirms the "is-ness" of human kind rather than its becoming." And a third statement by Albert Camus (1913-1960) states that "I revolt, therefore, I am." (Kurtzman, 1998, P. 189). Rumi considers Consciousness the main essence of human beings and all other beings. Thus, we could say "I am consciousness, therefore, I am." Our physical body and mental system are temporary residence for the trapped consciousness to experience the world through us. Our thoughts, beliefs, excitements or emotions are characteristics of mental self within the mental system.

Sources of Emotions

The main sources of excitements or emotions according to Rumi are within our mental system and the tendencies of our mental self which concentrates on psychological time of the past and present. On one hand, people who try to live in the past and become attached to the events of the past concentrate on the old pains and sufferings and they develop the major emotions of sadness, anger and depression. This happens for two reasons: One reason is that they can't let go of the negatively, perceived events of the past and the associated painful experiences and, the other reason is that past is only a mental concept and is not based on reality at present, consequently, they can't go back and change anything. They become attached and co-identified with the old pains and then, develop emotions and feelings such as sense of helplessness, hopelessness and worthlessness as well as negative and sad mood, resentment, and lose their interest in regular daily activities, lose their concentration and attention in life. that are characteristic symptoms of depression.

On the other hand, people who live in the future and are co-identified and attached to the imaginary, perceived, and probable upcoming events of the future, becomes quickly disappointed, because the future is also a mental concept and is not based on any reality at present. Thus, living in the artificial concept of future, which is unknown, causes the negative excitements and constant fear, anxiety and worries. There are two main reasons for developing these types of emotions as related to living in the future and becoming co-identified with the future: (1) Fear of something unknown that may happen in the future that mental self could not control according to his/her illogical expectations, and (2) the fear of losing what people possess such as material and non-material belongings, money, position, job, reputation, etc.

Rumi believes that all of our negative and exaggerated emotional excitements are caused by our mental self when we react to a situation, event or condition. It does not matter if the event is neutral or not, our mental self turns any neutral event into a negative one by negatively perceiving the event and personalizing or generalizing the event and then becoming attached to the events. Our excitements or emotions usually originate within our mental system by mental self, engaging in cognitive distortion and thinking errors that in turn leads to negative emotions and excitements and finally may lead to an inappropriate and abnormal behavior. A mental self with a negative thought or beliefs, may use anything as an excuse to become emotional either getting angry or becoming depressed. These excuses could be social, physical environmental stimuli or some internal impulses or stimuli which could cause negative and impulsive reaction for mental self. The internal impulses or stimuli relates to our thought process of building up stress and anger by using distorted concepts or statements such as "other peoples are threats," "rules have been violated, " " no one likes me," "people don't care about me, "life is unfair or unjust."

Our mental system is a mental, physical and emotional system. All these systems are transitory and perishable systems which could have both positive and negative functions. But our consciousness is eternal and unlimited. We would be better off if we could let our consciousness to be our lead which helps us to be at peace with ourselves and others and have a positive, productive and close relationships with others. Human emotions or excitements are usually manifest itself as tendencies of mental self to get excited by engaging in the wrong thinking and believing and then developing negative emotions which finally leads to wrong actions or unusual behaviors. If we try to interact with other people through our mental system and mental self our relationship with other people would become dysfunctional. Our awareness of external and internal world is achieved by the vibration of energy of light and consciousness within us that is the main motivating power of our positive emotions.

Human emotions or excitements are either being internalized and turn into depression and other related emotional problems or may be externalized and turn into different forms of aggression and violence. The internalized emotions or excitements can turn into externalized emotions and vice versa at any time depending on the needs of mental self. Human affect, mood and emotional state are based on the level of excitement mental self, wishes to obtain, which affects our behaviors. Most behaviors exhibited by mental self are the result of pain producing tendencies of mental self. People who do not have coping skills and are under the influence of their mental self are not able to deal with stressful situations, usually impulsively react with high intensity emotions and inappropriate behaviors. People may react to different internal or external stimuli or triggers by defending, resisting, withdrawing, or arguing, verbally or physically attacking other people depending on the tendencies of their mental self. Anger also may occur in the form of what Freud called "Displaced anger" or threatening impulses that may be directed toward another person, an animal or an object. Anger may range from low intensity of simple irritation to the high intensity of rage and violence.

Emotion includes four major components: First, reaction to external environmental or internal environmental stimulus, Second, Physiological response or activity as a reaction to environmental stimuli through our nervous system, Third, Personal or subjective feelings related to our sensual experience, and Fourth, Expression of those feelings. Stimulus can be either real or imagined. Emotions occur in response to both real and imagined stimuli. When we become emotional that is when our mental self, starts acting out, our limbic system and hypothalamus activate the autonomic system and causes autonomic arousal including physiological changes such as changes in our heart rate, blood pressure, and blood circulation. Any time we experience negative feeling a personal or subjective feeling usually accompanies our emotions. Descartes (1649) defined emotions as the passions of the soul. An emotion may be expressed the same way or differently in different cultures as learned behaviors. Emotions may be internalized and turn into depression or externalized and turn into anger and aggression.

The following emotional model of mental system shows the path of the development of emotions and the related consequences.

Mental System _____ develops mental Self
Mental Self _____ Produces thoughts, beliefs and excitements
Social/Physical Environment _____ produces events, incidents, situations and conditions

| Mental self reacts negatively | social/ physical environment events, incidents situations and conditions | Negative thoughts Cognitive Distortion | Inapp. Emotions (rage, fear, Jealousy, etc.) |

Figure.1 The Emotional Model of Mental System

As the emotional model represents, mental system produces mental self through human interaction with others. Mental self is the source of and produces our thoughts, beliefs, opinions and emotions and excitements. Events, incidents, situations, and conditions are happening within our social/physical environment. Our mental self has a habit of impulsively reacting to those events, incidents, situations and conditions and produces negative thoughts or cognitive distortion, which in turn produces our inappropriate emotions and excitements such as anger, rage, aggression, fear, depression, etc. In order not to create all those negative emotions or excitements, we should stop reacting impulsively and instead respond to those events, incidents, situations and conditions based on careful analysis and interpretation of any event or situation.

We can become addicted to our emotions or excitements. Our emotions are very complex and are guides to our behavior and could have adaptive functions. Emotions could have positive or negative functions. Emotion of pleasure will help us to repeat a behavior that was rewarded and produced pleasure in the past and escape a behavior that was associated with punishment or negative consequences. Emotion of fear helps us to stay away from dangerous situations or dangerous people or animals. Emotions then, not only motivates behavior, it also maintain the behavior in the future. Like instincts, emotions have an innate component. Feelings and thinking are not separated processes but two aspects of the same process within our mental system. The main difference between thinking and feeling is that thinking is mostly based on logical and objective reasoning but feelings are based on illogical and subjective reasoning. Feelings could never occur without thinking associated with it. Human emotions and excitements patterns are universal and occur regardless of culture or society. Emotions are expressed by people similarly in different cultures, however, the intensity of the emotions and the related behavioral responses or styles of showing emotions may vary from one culture to the next.

The best indicator of human emotion is facial expression and body movement, however, human voice also adds to our understanding of other people's emotions. Our emotional reactions or response relates to our mental system and mental self and the way our mental self has been conditioned and co-identified with the external stimuli. Our emotional reactions are automatic and are related to our nervous system and senses. Our nervous system generally reacts to different environmental stimuli and produces the emotions that are related to those stimuli based on the history of our behaviors. For example, if we are dealing with a threatening or dangerous situation, our nervous system in coordination with our glands produces the required hormones such as adrenalin to make us hyperactive and sends more bloods to our extremities such as hands and feet so that either we could take a fight stance or flight stance or reaction. The emotion of fear motivates us to escape the dangerous situation and the emotion of rage and anger motivate us to fight when there is no possibility of escape. Emotions thus, "are the internal bodily states of arousal that may influence our behavior in positive or negative ways." (Silverman, 1985, P. 258).

Emotional dimension of human being is a major determinant of human behavior. Human can both act and react emotionally to either internal or external stimuli. The intensity of human emotional response or reaction varies along a continuum ranging from mild sadness to intense sorrow or from mild happiness to manic excitement. Human earlier responses during the childhood are simple and undifferentiated, however, as human matures, he/she is able to engage in more complex and differentiated responses. Human emotions are either automatic naturally based on human instincts, or in reaction to external stimuli or a combination of both. Emotions can be conditioned based on the social and physical environmental conditions.

Emotion in the field of psychology concentrates on individual human being and his/her emotional patterns but in the field of sociology, the main emphasize is on the powerful influence of emotions as motivational force in the stability and change of social organizations, cultures and societies. Emotion is also important topic in the field of sociology where societies, cultures and social organizations are studied as related to emotions. Emotions are also of main concern in social psychology where main attention is on the emotional patterns of the small groups, crowd, mobs, gangs, etc. Scheff (2000) emphasized on the attention sociologists paid to the power of human emotions as related to changes in society.

There are three major sources of emotions: (1) Emotions in response to external environmental stimuli, (2) Emotions in response to internal stimuli, and (3) Emotions in response to unachieved motivations. There are many external social or physical stimuli that may be considered as disturbing stimuli to human beings' mental self. These stimuli could include negative social events such as wars, political, economic, and religious conflicts, deaths of loved ones, poverty, terminal illnesses of loved ones, etc. or negative and destructive natural disasters such as tornadoes, storms, floods, earthquakes, high level of noise and environmental pollutions, etc. Internal stimuli could act as disturbing stimuli causing many negative emotions. Example of internal stimuli are negative thinking, neurological problems, physical pain and discomfort, chemical and hormonal imbalances, diseases, psychological and mental statuses, etc. Our unachieved or unmet motivations and needs can also lead to many negative emotions. In general being frustrated, oppressed, exploited, attacked and rejected is a major source of many emotions.

The current empirical evidence suggests that emotional states results from complex interactions among several dimensions including cognitive, behavioral, biochemical, neuro-physiological, perceptual, and phenomenological factors. The Rational-Emotive Therapy (RET) of Ellis (1962), Aaron Beck (1963, 1976) provides cognitive theory of emotions. Arnold (1960, 1970) and R.S. Lazarus (1968) considered emotions as related to a cognitive process of situational appraisal. According to Woolfolk, cognition is unquestionably a fundamental contributor to emotion, if not its primary basis." (Lazarus,1976, p. 61). Eysenck and Beech, (1971) and Wolpe (1958) considered emotional behaviors as conditioned responses to conditioned stimuli. James-Lange theory (James, 1890), and Mowrer (1950) considered emotion as a function of autonomic nervous system. Cannon (1927) proposed that specific autonomic response pattern is not sufficient source of emotionality. It should be combined with activities of the sympathetic and parasympathetic nervous system. Predisposing psychosocial, emotional, and developmental influences such as hypo-and hyper-sensory responsiveness, fears, stereotypic behaviors, exposure to toxins, and excitements all can induce different types of emotions in people.

Forms of Emotions or Excitements

There are two main forms of excitements: The First one is the original excitements that are inherent and are created by our original, real self or consciousness and relate to positive and constructive excitements that makes us happy and joyful. And the second one is artificial mental excitement which is artificial, troublesome and destructive tendencies of our mental self. Mental self in general is an exciting seeking artificial being. Seeking excitement may occur in two different ways: One way is engaging in high intensity emotions and exaggerated emotional behaviors, and the other one is engaging in low intensity emotional behaviors. Excitement seeking mental self, experience excitement twice. First, during the performance of emotional behavior whether it occurs with high intensity or low intensity and the second time by talking about it and re-experiencing the similar sensations.

Emotions can be manifested in two Forms, overt or covert. The overt emotion includes the way individuals express their feelings state by talking about their feelings or what we can observe from their facial expressions and body movements. The covert emotions are internal bodily reactions and the subjective feelings associated with them that other people are not able to observe from outside the individuals physical system. Emotions are natural instinctual reactions or responses to environmental stimuli or are based on our attitudes, beliefs, thought processes as well as reaction or response to our internal sensory stimulation at any given point in time. The way we show our emotions relate to our life history and the history of learned behaviors from our parents, significant others and other people either from our direct contact with them or from watching movies and observing how people in the movies emotionally react or respond to different situations. Based on our history of conditioning and reinforcement we may express some emotions more frequently than others or with different intensity than others. Based on both hereditary and environmental contingencies and learned emotional and behavioral patterns, we may show similar emotional responses or reactions with members of our family.

Feelings are the result of neurological activities combined with the sensitivity of our senses that provide raw data and information to the brain and then, brain or our mental system changes these raw data or feelings and sensations into a processed and analyzed data in form of emotions. Feelings are physical, neurological and sensual experiences such as thirst, hunger, pain, discomfort, etc. Feelings "are physical sensations within the body such as warmth, tension, pulsation, pleasure, pain, flow, and motion; they may occur at the visceral, muscular, vascular, surface, or any other level of the body. They are part of the striving for homeostasis. When feelings (Somats) are evaluated and interpreted, at any level of consciousness, the process becomes an emotion." (Bernet, 1996, P. 3).

Attachment, Codependency and Co-identification

Attachment, codependency and co-identification with the material and non-material components and elements of this external world are the natural tendency and main characteristic of our mental self which operates within our mental system. The first perceived sin of human being was committed by the first two human beings Adam and Eve who are symbolically considered the main ancestors of all humans. The sin was using their mental system and developing their mental self and becoming co-identified and attached by the worldly materials such as the forbidden fruit or wheat representing the material things of the world. Before becoming attached and co-identified with worldly materials and things, they were within the realm of unity through their consciousness. Their body was made of minerals of the earth but their soul, spirit, light system of energy was made of formless, timeless, limitless consciousness. At first they were interdependent with life, consciousness, the universe and with each other. But as soon as they began to develop their mental self and using their mental system, they developed a sense of ownership, control, and power over each other and nature, they lost their independence and became codependent, co-identified and attached with each other and with the worldly objects. Becoming co-identified and attached to the worldly things, Adam and Eve created a barrier between themselves and their consciousness or their origin.

According to Rumi since the time human being became imprisoned within their sinful heart and mental system, their mental self, began using their limited reason and logic instead of the power of love that is the main power to unite all humans with their origin. After thousands of years, human now, is aware of their mistakes of over-using their mental system, which separated humans from their origin. This separation caused a situation that humans became addicted using their mental system and mental self and became too involved with variety of distracting affairs, forgetting why they are here on this planet and what their obligations are. Attachment and co-identification with the worldly material and non-material things and overusing our mental system are responsible for us developing all kinds of painful emotions and excitements.

Identity Crisis

Rumi believes that people become aware of their identities through the eyes of other people and the way other people see them. Thus, we should be like a clear mirror to reflect the picture of the other person without any distortion, judgement or reaction. This will help us to become aware of our true identity instead of the artificial identity we acquire through different interactions with others. As mental selves we try to put a mask to hide our true identity by playing roles and pretending to be someone who we really are not. Like Rumi, Shakespeare also declared that world is like a theater stage and people are the players within the world theater. Everyone tries to put up a show to present an ideal self that may not be their true self. Since the mental self is a mental construct and is constantly changing, it is hard for many people to know who they really are at any moment. Their concept of self is what other people reflect to them as a mirror. Thus, rapidly changing mental self along with constant and continuous change of all other human dimensions including environmental changes, will create confusion and identity crisis for mental selves.

Emotional Motivating Power

Mental self has a tendency to seek intense degree of need for emotional and physical stimulation and usually engages in various risky physical activities and affairs to receive different types of exciting stimulation. Mental self is unable to control sensation and excitement seeking impulses which causes trouble all the time. Emotions and excitements are loaded with energy that is fueled by our hormones such as adrenalin, beta-endorphin, and serotonin. Emotional power is rhythmic and can increase or decrease based on our internal emotional state and emotional reasoning. Emotional rhythm and excitements are associated with our heart beats and pulses and can have either positive or negative effects. Emotions such as love, affection, compassion, sense of empathy or sympathy are caused by positive emotional rhythms. Fear, anxiety, depression, mood instability, feelings of being persecuted or oppressed, feelings of being rejected or isolated, feelings of low self-esteem, low self-image and low self-regards or respects are caused by negative emotional rhythms. The main source of our positive or negative emotions and excitements are our thought processes within our mental system by our mental self that originate emotions.

Mental self with tendency to produce pain causes negative emotions through negative thinking and our real, objective self or consciousness produces positive emotions such as love, tranquility and creativity. Our internal consciousness keeps us aligned and at peace with ourselves, others and the whole universe. Concentrating on our consciousness, we seek the comfort of internal balance but concentrating on our mental self with inconsistency of our thought, belief and excitement systems, endanger our internal equilibrium. Mental self being an artificial existence produces internal conflict and sufferings. As long as human being is not able to resolve his/her internal conflict, would continue experiencing pains and confusions. A depressed mental self is not able to concentrate on real life situation and would not be able to be creative or productive being due to lack of positive motivation. The emotional rigidity of the mental self of a depressed human causes inflexibility and intolerance of ordinary life situations.

Emotions and excitements always are associated with motivating power whether positively or negatively. Our internal states of excitements particularly the excessive desires and wants or greed that are produced by our mental self which is never satiated, usually direct our behaviors. Human basic needs and desires are normal as long as it is related to human survival, but mental self has many types of artificial and distorted needs that are not real needs of human beings.

Classifications of Emotions or Excitements

Emotions have been classified in different ways: however, there is consensus that all emotions can be divided into two major groups: (1) Primary or basic emotion and (2) Secondary emotion. A primary emotion is what we feel right away at any point in time. But the secondary emotion is an outcome of the primary emotion and is being developed by our mental self. For example anger, fear, and depression are based on primary emotions such as helplessness, worthlessness and hopelessness as well as feeling rejected, isolated and neglected which produce the secondary emotion of depression. In order to understand secondary emotions, we need to identify what are the related primary emotions or raw feelings behind them.

Most of human behavioral excesses and deficits are related to our mental processes within our mental system and the mental self's inability to moderately express the secondary emotions. When we are not able to identify, analyze and express our primary feelings moderately, we are responsible for contributing to the emergence of related high intensity secondary emotions. Then, we internalize a high volume of feelings that later turns into high intensity emotions and the related explosive behaviors. For example when we feel oppressed, cheated, insulted, pressured or disrespected, we may develop the secondary emotion of anger due to our inability to cope with our primary emotions. This anger in turn may be converted to either an aggressive and explosive behavior if it is externalized, or, stay inside our mental system and in the long run, it turn into depression.

Emotions have also been classified according to the perception or duality trait of our mental system and mental self and seeing everything in dyadic pairs, viewing all phenomena in our life as opposites or complementary such as externalized and internalized emotions; positive and negative emotions; appropriate and inappropriate emotions; motivated or unmotivated emotions; placed or misplaced emotions; dyadic and polarized or unidimensional and multi- dimensional emotions. Another classification of emotions and excitements relate to the intensity of emotions which are low, medium and high intensity emotions. Any classification based on the level of intensity of emotion is arbitrary. For example we may classify the emotion into high and low level or we may have scale of zero to ten or zero to five, etc. The other classification of our emotions relates to a combination of our primary or raw feelings and secondary or analyzed emotions which is considered mixed emotions. Descartes (1649) classified human emotions into six major primary emotions: Wonder, love, hatred, desire, joy, and sadness. He believed that other emotions are produced as a result of interaction among these six primary emotions. Spinoza (1677) presented a three dimensional model of emotions: desire, joy and sadness. "Our affects are divided into actions and passions, when the cause of an event lies in our own nature more particularly, our knowledge or adequate ideas then it is a case of the mind acting." (Stanford Encyclopedia of Philosophy, 2001)

Some intellectuals developed evolutionary theories of emotions (Darwin, 1872; Bridges, 1032; Osgood, 1952; Tomkins, 1962, 1982; Plutchick, 1962, 1980, 1982; Izard, 1971, 1977, 1984). They emphasized on the positive functions of emotions and believed that primary emotions are universal, adaptive and help us to adapt to our social environment. For example anger motivates us to take action and solve our interpersonal problems. Fear protects us from dangerous situations. Regret helps us to learn from our mistakes. Moderate greed helps us to accumulate food and resources that helps us and our family to survive. Guilt helps us to think and not to violate other people's rights. Moderate emotions may have some positive functions, but when mental self's emotions occur with high intensity, it will have negative and destructive consequences. The problem begins when our mental self, engages in high intensity emotions or excitements such as explosive anger and aggression or excessive fear of losing his/her life, material and non-material belongings, then, emotions become dangerous and may lead to destructive or criminal behaviors.

Bridges (1932) developed a classification system based on the sequence of emotional development in the child. According to him "emotions develop from each other in a fixed sequence, starting with the emotion of excitement at birth. By six months of age, the child's negative emotions progresses from distress, to anger, to disgust, and to fear. He believes that most of emotions are already developed during the child's first year of life." (Bridges, 1932, P. 324-341). Izard (1971) classified emotions based on a cross-cultural identification of several primary emotions that are communicated in a culturally universal way, by different facial expression. Thus emotions are used for early communication. These primary emotions included "interest-excitement, enjoyment-joy, surprise-startle, distress-anguish, disgust-contempt, anger-rage, shame-humiliation, and fear-terror. According to him, primary emotions are universal and other emotions are developed from mixture of these primary emotions." (Izard, 1971, P. 561-565)

Plutchick (2002) classified emotions under eight basic or primary emotions in his psycho-evolutionary theory including: "Anger-rage, fear-terror, disgust, sorrow-sadness-grief, joy-ecstasy, acceptance-greed, anticipation, and surprise-astonishment. He believed that each emotion varied in intensity and had a specific adaptive significance. To him, primary emotions were required for our survival." (2002, P. 349). Ekman, mentioned sixteen primary emotions: "happiness, surprise, relief, wonder, ecstasy, triumph, ambition, pride, victory, goodness, kindness, compassion, fear, anger, sadness, and disgust. He emphasized that many facial expressions for emotions are similar across cultures." (Ekman, 2003, PP. 6, 7).

Expression of Emotions

Emotions usually are expressed appropriately in a mild or moderate way if we do not hold or stuff our feelings. This is based on the assumption that appropriate release of emotion is a healthy process. If we use our mental self, internalize our negative feelings for a long time, there is a high probability that our negative feelings turns into high intensity and secondary emotions of depression, aggression and self-destruction or destruction of other people. If we try to externalize our stuffed negative feelings, it may turn into aggression or destructive behavior against others. However, appropriate and mild expression of emotions is beneficial and helps us to relax and stay healthy. For example crying is one mild and beneficial form of expressing negative emotions. "The belief that crying has positive effects is of ancient origin.

More than 2,000 years ago, Aristotle theorized that crying at a drama "cleanses the mind" of suppressed emotions by a process called catharsis. Catharsis is the reduction of emotional distress by releasing the emotion in controlled circumstances." (Ornstein, 1985, P. 449). Ornstein reviews several studies of the effects of crying as follows:

> Frey (1982) contends that "emotional crying is an eliminative process in which tears actually removes toxic substances from the body. Crying may "cleanse the mind" in a much more literal sense than even the catharsis theorists imagine... There is reason to think that emotional tears may perform a very important function in the maintenance of physical health and emotional balance." (Ornstein, 1985, P. 449).

Religious prayers, mourning and crying as a form of excitement has a positive function for the person who cries or mourns by reliving his/her emotional and mental pains. Moslem's crying during the month of "Moharram," and during the religious lectures related to the massacre of Imam Hussein (the Shia-at Moslem Leader) and his relatives and friends by Bani Ommayed tribe in Karbala, Iraq, has a similar function. It is helpful to think of emotions as ranging on a continuum from low through medium to high intensity. To experience low intensity of emotion are healthy and will not lead to maladaptive behavioral or psychological problems. However, experiencing and intensifying our emotions to a high level of severity or repressing and internalizing our emotions may have serious negative and destructive consequences. "The goal is balance, not emotional suppression; every feeling has its value and significance. Thus, to manage emotions is to express them in an appropriate manner and not let them run out of control". (Goleman, 1998).

Theories of Emotions

Two major theories of emotions are: (1) Darwin's theory, emphasizing the role of biologically determined factors in emotion and (2) Cognitive theory of emotion, the view that emotion depends on how we appraise or evaluate a situation. Darwin believed that the way people express fear, anger, and other emotions is, inherited and universal. According to him emotions have survival value and communicative properties as well as inherited and biologically determined. Darwin influenced several modern theorists such as Izard (1977), Tomkins (1981), Plutchik (2001), James (1884, 1890), Cannon (1927, 1929), Eckman (1972) and Bard (1928, 1934).

According to William James (1884), emotion was the feeling or perception of those bodily changes that occur when one responds to a stimulus. Carl Lang (1885) also independently formulated the same idea that emotion was the feeling and perception of bodily changes that occur in response to an event or stimuli. According to James-Lang theory of emotion, the subjective experience of emotion results from the feedback one receives from the body, particularly the autonomic nervous system. The perception of one's own feelings or body responses makes us aware of our emotions. "The Schachter-Singer theory (1962) suggests that the emotions that we report to ourselves or to others result from the way in which we interpret our states of arousal…" (Silverman, 1985, p. 285).

Emotions similar to our thoughts and logics are our internal guidance system, which alert us when our basic needs are not met. For example, according to Maslow's (1943, 1972) hierarchy of needs, all humans have basic emotional needs such as the need to be loved, accepted or approved. If our need for approval and acceptance has not been met, we feel rejected or when our need for food and water has not been met we feel our life is threatened. When emotional needs are not met people become frustrated and engage in different types of inappropriate behaviors. Our emotional needs are based on our value system and priorities. Thus not all people have the same exact emotional needs. Emotions are means of communication, motivation, choice making, social relationship building, and in general a motivating force for our connection with other people and survivals. Emotions are not developed by themselves. They are rather a reaction or response to a variety of internal or external stimuli.

According to Izard (1977), "emotion is a reaction to either internal stimuli such as a memory, image, thought or another emotion or a reaction to external stimuli which causes a change in nervous system activity." Thus emotion is a reflexive reaction to a stimulus. According to these theorists emotion can be activated and experienced without cognition. The behavior interruption theory of emotion holds that "emotion is functionally useful as a signal of progress toward goals, with negative emotions indicating less-than-expected progress and positive emotions adequate or better-than-expected progress." (Carver & Scheier, 1990, PP. 19-35)

Cognitive Aspects of Emotions or Excitements

The cognitive theories of emotion considers emotions primarily in terms of their associated cognitions, and proposes that, in order to have emotion, one must have some type of beliefs or attitude toward something to begin with. Major proponents of cognitive theory of emotions are : Beck (1976, 1963), Ellis (1994, 1977, 1962) Lazarous (1991), Schachter-Singer (1962), Joel Marks (1982), Oakley (1992), Broad (1971), Lyons (1980), Solomon (1980), Neu (2000), and Nussbaum (2001). The schachter-Singer theory of emotion (1962) "emphasizes the role of cognition in emotion and asserts that our perception and interpretation of internal arousal will determine the intensity and types of emotion we develop." Our attitudes about our emotions affect our behavior in different ways. For example an optimistic point of view may lead to emotional, psychological and physical health, while a pessimistic point of view may lead to emotional, psychological and physical illness. Negative emotions may also lead to mental and physical illnesses.

According to the cognitive theorists, a stimulus can't create an emotional response unless we consider that stimulus to be dangerous or harmful.

"Whether or not physiological arousal becomes emotion depends on a cognitive evaluation of the situation that caused the arousal. The theory holds that emotion depends on two factors: an internal state of arousal and an appropriate cognition with which to label that state." (Schachter-Singer two Factor Theory (1962),

While Lazarous (1991) believes that cognition comes first and emotion comes next, Zajonc (1984) believes emotion comes first and then cognition occurs. But the commonly held belief is that cognitive processing influences emotions and emotions in turn impact cognitive processing. Emotions are feelings that are related to some type of mental experience and are constantly in a state of flux. Our emotions are related to our mental self who constantly moves from the past to present, or from the present to the perceived future experiences. Emotions are also contagious based on our empathy or sympathy for other people. Even the contagious aspect of emotions is through observational learning and development of similar emotions. Emotion is a cognition which is in relation to some aspects of our physiological, neurological, and hormonal activity that I call "emotional rhythm." Our emotional rhythm may range from positive to negative or from low to high level based on the acquisition or lack of meeting our basic needs. Cognitive theorists believe that emotion depends on how we appraise or evaluate a situation.

One of the cognitive theorists, Lazarus (1991) believed that people must first interpret the event in terms of its effect on well-being; that is, they must come to a cognitive appraisal of the event. Cognitive activity is considered to be necessary precondition for emotion. The higher the level of knowledge and information about our environment, the less intensity of our emotions will be. In order for us to be rational and make the right decision, we should have the right information. If we do not have enough information about something, we become anxious and emotional because we may not be able to make the right decision. However, if we have enough knowledge and understanding of our situation or condition, we may display mild emotional arousal.

Rumi believed that like fear any other emotion become intensified due to ignorance and lack of knowledge. It relates to fear of unknown, fear of dark and fear of confusion. Similar to Rumi, Simonov (1969), the Russian scientist believed that "emotions serve as a reserve mechanism when there is not enough information to act rationally and purposefully. He believes that there is an inverse relationship between emotion and knowledge." He offered a formula to show how our emotions are developed:

$E = -N (In -Ia)$
Emotion = - need for food, shelter, etc.
In = Information necessary to achieve need
Ia = Information available or acquired

Figure.2 Simonov Formula (1969)

Human emotion is not static. It changes constantly based on the changes in our social and environmental situations or conditions and the definition and interpretation of these situations or conditions. Emotions and moods changes so quickly that they do not provide an accurate basis for understanding other's behaviors across times and across situations. Human continuous appraisal of the changing situations will produce new types of emotions at any given time. Our first response to an environmental stimulus is arousal which is produced through appraisal of the situation. However, as we continue to engage in the reappraisal of the situation, we will be able to identify whether the situation is safe or dangerous and we develop the related emotions accordingly. Fogarty (2000) believes that "negative interpretation of a trauma such as a death of a loved one by a child often results in the bereaved child defining a normal grief reaction as abnormal, creating an emotional paradox..." (Fogarty, 2000, P. 8)

Emotions may have both positive and negative functions. Sometimes even emotional tension can be adaptive, motivating, and helping the individual to take the right action. Emotional tension is highly dependent on human subjective experience and the level of the emotional tension which may manifest itself in a positive way in the forms of joy or pleasure or in a negative way in the forms of fear, anxiety, or distress. Generally a moderate level of emotional tension is adaptive and productive in helping the individual to cope with problems. Both the extremely high and extremely low emotional tensions are pathological and harmful.

Rumi believes that events, incidents, situations and conditions may not be naturally bad it is the wrong appraisal, negative thinking and reaction to those events that makes them look bad to us. Some people make distinction between emotivism and cognitivism regarding our social or moral judgment. Emotivism was introduced by Ayer (1946) and refined by Stevenson (1963). According to emotivism, social or moral judgment is an expression of the appraiser's attitudes either positive or negative, toward the object of evaluation, rather than make judgement about the properties of that object. Cognitivism, on the other hand, holds that social or moral judgments should be considered as assertions about the moral properties of people, their activities, behavior, or any other characteristics of moral assessment.

Emotional Brain

The brain as the main tool of mental self within the mental system is the center of all of our emotions and our limbic system is largely responsible for many of our emotional reactions. Mental self utilizes our limbic system and impulsively react to any situation. A discussion of the relationship between the brain, nervous system and our behaviors is out of the capacity of this chapter where the main emphasis is on the relationship between our emotions, and our behaviors. However, it is important to know that the upper brain or new cortex is more responsible for rational and logical thinking and the limbic system or emotional brain is responsible for our emotional reactions and stresses. In an emergency situation, or under a real or imagined threat, the limbic system immediately responds through automatic nervous system and regulates the release of necessary hormones into the blood stream.

Different types of emotions could cause quite different forms of bodily reactions. Fear for example, stimulates the glands through the nervous system to send more blood to our feet to make it stronger for flight. Anger stimulates the glands to send more adrenalin into our hands to make our hands stronger for a fight. Facial expressions associated to different emotions are universally very similar. However, different people may show different types of emotional responses to the same situation. The differences among different people regarding their emotional responses may relate to their personal experiences, socialization and learned behaviors.

Some Psychologists and thinkers investigated the relationships between emotional brain or limbic system the producer of our emotional reactions and thinking brain or new cortex the center of our rational thoughts. Kolb & Milner, (1980); Safer & Leventhal, (1977); Koestler, (1974) analyzed the relationships between the brain and human emotions. According to them the left hemisphere responds to the verbal content of emotional expression and the right hemisphere responds to the tone and gesture. Other writers emphasized more on emotional intelligence. Robert Thorndike wrote about "social intelligence" in the late thirties. Howard Gardener discussed the "multiple intelligence', and proposed that "intrapersonal", and interpersonal intelligences are as important as the type of intelligence typically measured by IQ and related test (Cherniss, 2000). However, the Phrase "emotional intelligence", was coined in 1990 by a Yale psychologist, Peter Salovy, and John Mayer, also a psychologist from the university of New Hampshire to describe certain qualities, for example, understanding one's own feelings, empathy for the feelings of others, and the regulation of emotion in way that enhances living (Salovy, P; Mayer, J.D, 1990). According to Salovy and Mayer, " emotional intelligence is a type of social intelligence that involves the ability to monitor one's own and other's emotions, to discriminate among them, and to use the information to guide one's thinking and action" (Salovy, 1993, P 433). The foundation of emotional intelligence is self-knowledge. It involves awareness of emotions; or self-awareness, an ability to manage those emotions; or self-regulation, and self-motivation (Wood and Wood, 2000).

Goleman (1995), extending the work of Salovy and Mayer (1990) and Howard Gardener separated the components of emotional intelligence into: (1) Intrapersonal component, (2) Interpersonal component. Intrapersonal intelligence is a correlative ability, turned inward. Interpersonal intelligence is the ability to understand other people; what motivates them, how they work, and how to work cooperatively with them. Goleman's emotional competence framework classifies emotional intelligence into five major components:

"(1) Self-awareness or knowing one's internal states, preferences, resources, and intuitions, (2) Self-regulation, or managing one's internal states, impulses, and resources, (3) Motivation or emotional tendencies that guide or facilitate reaching goals, (4) Empathy or awareness of others feelings, needs, and concerns, and (5) Social skills or ability to handle relationships successfully and adeptness of inducing desirable response on others." (Goleman D., 1995).

Emotional intelligence is the ability to sense and use emotions to more effectively manage ourselves and influence positive outcomes in our relationships with others. An emotion usually originates as a result of receiving different types of sensory stimulation from the external environment or from the internal cognitive stimulation. These feelings may be pleasant or unpleasant. Based on how we define, analyze, or interpret those external and internal stimulations or information/input, we may then make decision and then take an action. Therefore, our life is thus affected to a large extent by both our thinking and feelings or emotions. Our thinking is source of our emotions and our emotions in turn motivates our thinking and decision making process which finally will lead to our behavior or action. There is a reciprocal relationship between emotion and cognition. As Daniel Goleman, elegantly put it, "in the dance of feeling and thought, the emotional faculty guides our moment-to-moment decisions, working hand-in-hand with the rational mind, enabling or disabling thought itself." (Goleman, 1998).

An error from objectively based thinking are less frequent, less severe, and easier to correct than are errors from emotionally based thinking. Our mode of thinking influences the content of our thinking, emotions and our behavior. Cognitive theorists believe that mental functions such as thinking, perception, consciousness, and memory cause our emotions. However other theorists consider emotions as motivators of our mental functions. Zajonc (1980, PP. 151-175) argues that "mental functions are most often in the service of emotions, not the reverse: that we evaluate first and think of the reasons secondly..." (Ornstein, 1984, P. 453).

Emotional Stress

Stress cluster include negative emotions that we develop when we are stressed out as related to our daily life activities. It includes negative feelings such as stressed, tormented; tortured; and distressed. Stress has been defined in many ways. It is a complex, dynamic process of interaction between a person and his or her life. It is an unpleasant state of emotional and physiological arousal that people experience in situations that they perceive as dangerous or threatening to their well-being. Stress results from failure to adequately cope with stressor. "Stress occurs when the internal responses of the individual to pressure are experienced as excessive." (Silverman,1985, p. 394).

Stress has physical and emotional effects on us and can create positive or negative feelings. The positive effect of stress is that it motivates us to take action. It can provide us with new form of awareness and an exciting new perspective. The negative effect of stress is that it can lead to other emotional states such as distrust, rejection, anger, aggression and depression or to physical symptoms such as headaches, hypertension, peptic ulcers, hypo-thyroid and hyper-thyroid problem. Stressors could be either internal or external. Internal stressors are associated with physiological, biological, neurological, glandular and hormonal as well as cognitive, emotional, psychological, and developmental factors.

Several factors including physiological, biological, neurological, emotional, cognitive glands, hormones, as well as social and ecological factors are responsible for producing stress in our life. Physiological factors include physical disabilities and limitations; abnormalities in the sexual arousal and tension; unmet basic needs such as hunger, need to go to the bathroom, clothing, sensory stimulation, cleanliness, and other basic physical needs such as addiction, dietary restrictions, and heightened physiological arousal such as pain and physical discomfort, and other physical sensitivities. Biological stressors include genetic factors or chromosome abnormalities, hereditary factors, puberty, menstruation, and menopause in women. Neurological stressors including neurotransmitters involved in the induction and enhancement of our negative emotions such as anger and aggression. Organic brain syndrome, neurological damage or head injury, frontal lobe impairment leading to intermittent periods of irritability that escalate into an emotional response and diminished coping skills such as anger and impulsivity.

Hormonal factors could also cause different kinds of stress. Chemical Imbalance in the brain is associated with variety of stresses. For example, a little or too much amount of hormones such as testosterone, progesterone, beta-endorphin, nor-epinephrine, dopamine, epinephrine, and serotonin could cause emotional stress or distress. Medical and medication side effects could cause different forms of stress. Psychological and other emotional factors are also considered as main source of the stress and vise-a versa. Cognitive factors could also create a great deal of stress which in turn leads to different forms of behavioral consequences.

Our negative thoughts, perceptions, and attitudes could cause varieties of stresses for us. The way we think, will determine how we feel and, how we act? If we define our situation in a negative way, then we develop negative emotions and stress which may lead to inappropriate behavior. Communication factors are also important in causing stress related behaviors. Inability to communicate our wishes, wants, and needs as well as our physical or emotional pain and discomfort can cause a high degree of stress. Emotional and developmental factors could also lead to a high level of stress.

External social and ecological environmental factors are also considered a major source of stress. Stressors are largely product of their environment. Thus it is important to identify the environmental sources of stress. Social environmental factors include over-crowding; high level of noise; direct or indirect provocation from others such as physical,; sexual, and verbal abuse and threats; interruption in individual's daily routines; sudden transition or change in our daily life; major change in our job or work schedules; having a limited range of options; negative attitudes of others; negative situations or conditions; witnessing other people misery; oppression and misfortune; competing with others in many areas of life; lack of emotional and financial support; not being able to control our destiny or future; negative significant events in our life, and conflict and power struggles.

External physical environment such as lighting patterns; noise level from industries, factories, transportation vehicle, etc.; environmental temperature; inadequate ventilation inside the buildings; air pollutions; exposure to environmental toxins and lack of space are also major sources of stress. Silverman (1985) divides stressors into five major categories:

> (1) Biological deprivation, or interference with the satisfaction of some bodily need. (2) Danger, real or imagined. (3) Threats to self-esteem. (4) Stimulus overload, which results from too many demands from the environment. (5) Developmental change which include stresses that accompany the social and personal development of the individual. To deal with stress, it is important to learn how to deal with stress than to try to eliminate it.

II

Externalized Human Emotions: Excessive and Exaggerated Emotions

"On the day of death, when my bier is on the move, do not suppose that I have any pain at leaving this world. Do not sweep for me, say not "Alas, Alas!" You will fall into the devil's snarc__ that would indeed be alas! When you see my hearse, say not "Parting, Parting!" That time there will be for me union and encounter. When you commit me to the grave, say not "Farewell, Farewell!" For the grave is a veil over the reunion of paradise. Having seen the going-down, look upon the going-up; how should setting impair the sun and the moon? To you it appears as setting, but it is a rising; the tomb appears as prison, but it is release of the soul. What seed ever went down into the earth which did not grow? What bucket ever went down and came not out full? Why this complaining of the well by the Joseph of the spirit? When you leave closed your mouth on this side, open it on that, for your shout of triumph will echo in the placeless air." (Rumi, 118) Translated by Arberry, 1968.

Some people have tendencies to continually stuff negative emotions and save it for later. This tendency creates a major problem for mental self when something goes wrong and mental self, emotionally reacts to the situation by externalizing the stuffed emotions and causing variety of explosive behaviors.

First mental self internalizes different emotions and stuff those emotions that does not want to deal with at the moment. While mental self, maintain these negative emotions inside, the main consequence is feeling sad and depressed. But being weak it is not possible to hold them for an extended time period. Thus, when mental self is not able to stuff more emotions due to its limited capacity, suddenly engages in aggressive or destructive behaviors. Externalized human emotions and the related behaviors include: Anger, control, power and oppression; aggression, war, and fight: vengefulness, hate and ownership: verbal abuse clusters such as verbal labeling and mislabeling, stereotyping, false accusation, and dehumanization and demonization.

Anger Cluster

Anger

Anger is a perfectly normal reaction for mental self and it emerges when the events are occurring in a way that the expectations of mental self are not met. However, if mental self becomes angry, it is better to release the anger moderately by not using high intensity emotional words such as hate. It is better to say "I am not satisfied, pleased, or comfortable," instead of saying "I am furious, hateful or mad" which are high intensity words. Part of the problem is our self-image that mental self creates for us and when something happens that is against the expectation and approval of our mental self, we take it too seriously and make a big deal and intensify our emotions of hate and anger. Events by themselves are neutral but our evaluation and interpretation of events either in a positive way or negative way makes a big difference and either makes us happy or sad based on our own definition of the events. Problem arises when we hold grudges and not letting go of our anger which can either be internalized and lead to depression or it can be externalized and turn into aggression and violence.

Rumi (13th Century) consider anger as one of the wrong emotions we develop when we react impulsively and negatively to a neutral event or situation. If we do not react to different incidents, then there would not be a negative consequence related to any event. Novaco, (1977, P. 5) and (Novaco, 1976, P. 133) offered a cognitive-behavioral approach to the treatment of anger problems. Ellis1977, 1994) developed an ABCDE model of anger management where A stands for activating events, B represents belief system, C stands for emotional and behavioral consequences, D represents for Detecting, discrimination, and debating, and E stands for effect or future philosophy of anger.

Anger is an extremely active negative energy directed toward someone, something, or self. It may be a reactive response to a perceived injustice, oppression, or unexpected negative event. Anger cluster include negative feelings that we develop when we are angry at ourselves, others and events or situations. It include negative feelings such as aggravated, argumentative; nervous; bothered; bursting; provoked; quarrelsome; reckless; displeased; disturbed; resentful; annoyed; aroused; enraged; flared up; aggressive; boiling; pressured; furious; inflated; pissed off; rebellious; sullen; disappointed; bitterness; discouraged; destructive; resilient. Anger involves a sense of out-rage, frustration, conflict; irritation, or violent conflict. Anger may relate to internal physical, emotional, psychological, neurological, hormonal factors or it may relate to external precipitating stimuli.

Anger is one of our natural emotions and we are created with this quality inherent in us. Therefore, we should not try to completely eliminate this emotion, but to restrain it within due limits so that, by avoiding the negative behavioral consequence, we may maintain our conduct within the norm of our society. Anger is one of many feeling we experience and an emotional error which may occur with different intensity (i.e., low, medium, and high). Feelings are energy which moves freely from inside us to the outside world and back again. Sometimes people learn to internalize their anger as a way of trying to control their feelings when they become intense. Internalizing anger is holding it in, squishing it down inside us, shutting down emotionally, and pretending that we are really not angry. However, internalizing our anger only makes the anger worse.

Anger also occurs in response to emotions of threat or fear. Anger is a learned behavior. How we go about experiencing anger, expressing it, and coping with it however, is learned by watching our significant others, or role models. Our parents, teachers, relatives, friends and others are role models for our emotional self. Anger will not become a problem as long as we can use angry words with low intensity such as impatient, dismayed, disgusted, etc. When we are using angry words with high intensity such as furious, enraged, hatred, etc., we develop high intensity emotion of anger. Anger is one of the correlates of maladaptive, deviant, and criminal behavior.

Mental selves with high intensity of anger could become very aggressive and dangerous. They become very competitive in sport or driving or jealous of other peoples over a variety of things. They become very competitive in many areas of life when upset. They become highly sensation seeking, irritable, hostile and assaultive. Their emotional instability provides them with a poor sense of control. The angry mental self, experiences anger with such frequency and intensity that causes problems for self and others. Anger when stuffed for an extended period of time becomes like a time bomb ready to explode at any time. This type of chronic anger can turn into major explosive episode if mental self highly react to an unpleasant situation or condition. It begins with an isolated episode, but it will be repeated over and over based on the situation and mental self's reaction to the situation.

Mental self utilizes the internal stuffed anger to control others. The consequence of anger is that the individual harms self and others. Sometimes, mental self uses anger to keep other people quiet and get them of his/her back. "The criminal experiences anger with such frequency and intensity that it has serious repercussions for himself and others. Anger, though pervasive in the criminal, is not always shown. Anger is a mental state that is sometimes expressed outwardly, but more often boils within. It is most dangerous when it is not on the surface." (Samenow, and Yochelson, 1993, p.268).

Conflict as an emotion arises when our interests are incompatible with other people's interests. Rumi believes that the main conflict exist between our mental self which is a source of all of our negative emotions and excitements and our consciousness that is the source of joy and tranquility. Human is responsible to create a balance between the positive and negative functions of mental self. The positive function is that mental self accumulates so much pain and suffering that we try to deactivate or reduce the mental self's negative thoughts, beliefs and excitements. And try to keep our mental self as simple as possible. Another positive function of our mental self is to receive, analyze, classify, generalize, store or delete information and data that we receive through our sense organs and help us to make better decision. The negative function of mental self, is producing constant negative and painful emotions, thoughts and beliefs, and making us co-identified and attached to these mental activities as well as material and non-material things of the external world.

One form of anger is frustration. Frustration "occurs when a person's drive to satisfy a certain need or achieve a certain goal is blocked." (Silverman, 1985, p. 403). Chronic frustration will lead to tension. Frustration as an emotion develops when we are not able to achieve a goal due to external conditions or when we have some internal limitation such as lack of skills, or coping mechanisms. Conflict "occurs when the individual's needs and goals are incompatible either with one another or with the demands that are placed on the individual" (Silverman, 1985, p. 405). Frustration is a natural tendency of mental self, because anything that is not based on mental self's expectation causes major frustration for him/her.

Aggression and Fight

Aggression and fighting is a major tendency of mental self to expand self and create a sense of existence. Aggression is any form of behavior under the influence of negative emotion directed toward the goal of harming or hurting another person who is either motivated to avoid such treatment or motivated to react and develop similar emotion. Aggression either is practical or intentional. If it is intentional it has the potential power to turn into action and harm someone. Whether a particular behavior is determined to be aggressive depends on many factors such as the characteristic of the aggressor, the intension of the aggressor, the intensity of the emotion behind the aggression, the intensity of the behavior itself, and finally the intensity of the assault and its physical and emotional effect. Most aggressions are related to the high intensity secondary emotions such as hate, revenge, greed, jealousy and fear and anxiety. Fear is a major cause of aggression like a cat that is cornered jumps and scratches people, a fearful person jumps and attack other people out of fear not out of courage.

There are many factors that are associated with aggressive behaviors. Social determinants of aggression such as socially learned aggressive behaviors, contagious aggression, fear-induced aggression, territorial defense or offense aggression, maternal protection aggression particularly in animals; Emotional determinants of aggression are anger and rage related aggression, Fear-induced aggression, aggression that relates to greed and possessing money, land, or luxuries from others; environmental determinants of aggression are air pollution, high level of noise, crowding and hot temperature. Situational determinants of aggression are aggressions that are related to no escape opportunities, Internal determinants of aggression such as heightened physiological arousal, sexual arousal, pain, thirst, hunger, hormones imbalances; Instinctive aggression or fighting instinct that human shares with animals; Neurological determinants of aggression are aggression related to brain abnormalities.

Wars

Mental selves being artificial transitory beings within human mental system try to establish themselves and make themselves known and survive they have to have other mental selves as escape-goats that they could quarrel with, fight with or as a group to go to war against each other. Mental selves could not feel important without having others to compare themselves and to have conflict with. It is through development of conflict and war that mental selves could feel strong and their existence more observable. Mental self enjoys creating conflict and gets their fuel from contrast and struggle with others. When mental selves create conflict, fight and war, it is the mental selves being highly active within our mental system and being under the influence of mental selves' thoughts, beliefs, perceptions, appraisal and interpretation emotions or excitements and the concept of duality of life which mental selves are using to have in-group and out-group, good and bad, angels and demons, friends and enemies, etc.

Without having some people to blame and demonizing them, mental selves could not create wars. First they have to find imaginative, artificial enemies, then to demonize them through negative labelling, convincing the in-group members of the common enemy or out group and then justifying the conflict and war against the artificially made enemies. This is the major emotional and cognitive distortion processes which mental selves are using to start a war and justifying the war. Stoessinger (1985) in his book entitled "Why Nations go to War," suggests some major precipitating factors in the outbreaks of war.

"The most important single precipitating factor in the outbreak of war is misperception. Such distortion may manifest itself in four different ways: in a leaders' image of himself; a leaders' view of his adversary's character; a leader's view of his adversary's intentions toward himself; and finally, a leader's view of his adversary's capabilities and power.." (Stoessinger, 1985, P. 207)

Revenge and Vengefulness

Vengefulness is another tendency of mental self, due to its resentment and holding grudges against other people. Vengefulness is a deep emotional state and is based on delaying and stuffing anger and trying to get back at another person later. It is also based on cognitive distortions and misinterpretation and wrong appraisal of the situation a mental self is coping with. Revenge is also based on learned behaviors because it is contagious and bad role models could teach it to other people. Most of the time the vengefulness or revenge comes to the surface when a mental self is becoming offended by an attack to his/her artificial authority, artificial reputation or chastity and a sense of injustice, oppression and being controlled by others. Mental self likes to have good name and positive reputation, thus any offense against his/her artificial reputation would become a narcissistic injury to him/her. "People who are more vengeful tend to be those who are motivated by power, by authority and by desire for status. They don't want to lose face." McKee, 2009, P. 34).

Hate

Hate is a high intensity negative emotion which is considered an opposite of love, a high intensity positive emotion. Hate can be based on fear of its object or a reaction to the past negative consequences of dealing with that object. Hate can be developed based on other feelings such as prejudice, envy and jealousy against another person, a group, a race, a religion, or a society. Hate or hatred "is an emotion of intense revulsion, distaste, enmity, or antipathy for a person, thing, or phenomenon; a desire to avoid, restrict, remove, or destroy its object."(Wikipedia, the Free Encyclopedia, 2004). This cluster includes negative feelings that we develop when we don't like ourselves, others, something and situation or event. It includes negative feelings such as hate; revengeful; etc. Hate is one of the major roots of negative emotions.

The behavioral consequence of hate is anger, aggression, assault, and destruction of others, self, and objects; Self- defeating and self-punishing behaviors such as self-injury, self-mutilation, suicide and para-suicides, social conflict, negative social relationships, depression and social isolations "Deprived of the affective nourishment to which they were entitled, their only resource is violence. The only path which remains open to them is the destruction of the social order of which they are the victims. Infants without love, they will end as adults full of hate." (Spitzer, 1975, PP. 826-845).

Disgust is a stronger feeling of dislike. This cluster relates to the unwanted emotion which typically is associated with events that are perceived as highly unclean, repugnant, abnormal, maladaptive, immoral, illegal, or unethical. Disgust is a reaction to a harsh treatment of an individual victim or a violent act by an aggressive individual. This cluster includes negative feelings that we develop when we try to break the law or violate the norm of the society. It includes negative feelings such as anti-social, mischievous;

fraudulent; phony; pretentious; promiscuous. Anticipation is an emotion cluster which includes both anxiety about upcoming positive events or worries about some upcoming negative events. It may give us pleasure in considering some expected pleasant events or irritation at expecting some negative events to happen. This emotion is mainly developed when we have to wait for something or deal with delays.

Power Cluster

Control, Power and Oppression

Mental self likes to control other people by using coercion and use of force if possible to get people do what he/she desires and expect from others. This tendency of mental self, relate to selfishness of the self which wants everything for him/herself. By controlling other people, mental self may use a deviant tactic of pretending he/she is really assisting, protecting and rescuing another person, but in fact he/she is dictating to others what they need to do and how to do it which is against other people independence and freedom. Mental self loves power and control and oppression is the consequence of using power to control other people life. In order for mental self to achieve this goal, he/she pretends to have imaginary power because that is the way mental self, perceive self. A person with rigid mental self uses pretention as a tool to fool people in thinking that he/she is doing others a favor and makes them to think that they owe him/her something. What mental self is using is brainwashing technic and try to redefine different situation in a way that he/she can make benefit from it. Through power and control mental self, tries to obtain prestige, attention and privileges.

Oppression includes emotions or feelings that we develop when we are disrespected, oppressed undignified. Negative Feelings under this cluster include; beaten down; cut down; criticized; dehumanized; disrespected; raped; humiliated; inferior; insulted; invalidated; labeled; lectured to; mocked; offended; put down; resentful; ridiculed; stereotyped; teased; and underestimated;

Suffocated; and suffered. Being oppressed is associated with suffering by any unwanted condition such as physical, emotional, or psychological pain and discomfort. Oppression includes emotions or feelings that is developed when we feel powerless and controlled. It include negative feelings such as imposed; bossed around; controlled; imprisoned; inhibited; forced; manipulated; obligated; over-controlled; over-ruled; powerless, pressured; coerced; restricted; intimidated; challenged; exploitative; inferior; manipulated; possessive; restricted; strangled; submissive; subordinated; and trapped.

Emotional Ambition

Ambition is an emotion which is highly associated with high self-esteem, grandiosity, and pride and can serve positive or negative function. Ambition is defined as "an eager, and sometimes an inordinate, desire for preferment, honor, superiority, power, or the attainment of something." (Webster's Dictionary, 1913). This cluster includes negative feelings that we develop when we feel we are better than others. It includes negative feelings such as ambition; arrogance; self-centered; selfish; narcissistic; stingy; and negative pride. According to Beck, problem with pride, contempt, and arrogance arise when we compare ourselves to others. "If we feel superior, then we place them in a lesser position, violating the principles of equality and justice… The feeling of pride can cause us to have a higher opinion of ourselves than we merit, and in comparison we may also believe others are lower than they deserve." (Beck, 2004, p. 8).

Ambition is not positive or negative by itself. It is simply a human emotion to motivate for achievement, fulfillment, and greatness. Ambition may serve positive or negative functions depending on our purpose. The positive form of ambition is called aspirations, which is desire for excellence, accomplishment, and advancement. The negative form of ambition is the major tendency of our mental self which is selfish ambition and includes thirst and un-satiable appetite for wealth, power, prestige, and status, and success whatever the price may be. Sometimes, individual's aspirations may turn into selfish ambitions when they are not successful in fulfilling their needs. This is due to frustrating effect of selfish ambition particularly when goal is not achieved or can't be achieved. In this situation individual is still thirsty for achieving the objective, however, the level of motivation is not high enough, because reality shows the goal is not achievable. Mental self has a tendency to have as much as possible without becoming satiated and as part of excessive wants, he/she likes to own others and material and non-material things. Ownership of other people is an extreme form of control which forces people to stay away from the controller.

Verbal Abuse Cluster

Labelling/Mislabeling
Labeling or mislabeling is a form of verbalized negative emotion and thought. It involves describing a person in a high intensity and emotionally loaded manner. It involves associating people with negative traits and characteristics to make them look bad or sinister. Labeling may be used against an individual person or it may be used against a group by generalizing a bad trait from a few individuals to the whole group, race or religion. Labeling or mislabeling is one form of emotional reasoning or thinking. The purpose of labeling or mislabeling is to put down other people or make them look bad. Accurate knowledge of other cultures or subcultures makes us more open minded and eliminates labeling or mislabeling.

Stereotyping
Similar to labeling and mislabeling, stereotyping is either based on intentional or unintentional association of people with negative traits or characteristic. The lack of knowledge and information about other people or ignorance is the main reason for stereotyping. Again stereotyping involves generalizing negative traits from a few people to the whole population. The main purpose of stereotyping is for our mental self, trying to show that we are better and more important than other people. By making them look bad we try to make ourselves better than them. To eliminate the stereotyping we need to increase our knowledge and information about other people.

Verbal assault or Threats

Verbal assault is one of the characteristic of mental self to bring other people down and make self, more strong and important. It is a form of verbalized negative emotion and thought. Verbal assault or threat involves applying a negatively loaded phrase or word to a person or to exaggerate on a person's deficiency. The intention is usually to put down another individual, to manipulate or control others, using words such as, jerk, dumb, idiot, stupid, etc. Verbal assault may also include verbal threats to scare and intimidate other people. Verbal assault or threats are neither socially appropriate nor legally acceptable. However, it only works against another person when the person who receives it has a rigid mental self and negatively reacts to the verbal assault or threats.

Preventive measure of ignoring the person, who engages in verbal assault or threats, reduces the negative power of assaultive person. But if we impulsively react to another person's verbal threats, it could have devastating effect on us. For the person who is weak and has a rigid mental self being under the continuous verbal threats or assaults, may lead to serious mental damage particularly for children. The long term effect of continuous verbal assault or threats can cause variety of mental and emotional damage for the person who is receiving the assault. Person may develop a sense of powerlessness, hopelessness, worthlessness which may lead to depression. The long term effect of mental and emotional abuse may produce psychosomatic symptoms and stress-related physical symptoms such as migraine headaches, ulcer, diabetes, thyroid dysfunctions, nervous twitches, etc.

False Accusation

Mental self has a tendency to produce pain for self and others and tries to discredit and create bad reputation for other people by providing and presenting unfavorable inaccurate information about them. It is a different form of verbal assault. The intention to provide unfavorable information is to create a negative reputation or bias people against a person or a group. Another intention of mental self to engage in false accusation is to distract people from his/her own shortcoming and faults and put all the attention on someone else. This negative activity also is employed by people who are competing against other people or candidates during pre-election time. A special form of false accusation is sarcasm a passive-aggressive statement or remarks mental self makes to put other people down. By putting other people down, mental self tries to have power over people and to control them.

Fault Finding

Mental self, consider self, as complete and superior to others thus, is not able to see his/her own faults and shortcomings, but, pays extra attention to other people and try to come up with any minor deficiencies to aggrandize and put them down. Fault finding involves a sense of superiority and perfectionism of the mental self as related to other people as being inferior and incomplete. It is also escaping from self-fault by seeing fault in other people. Rumi provides several verses of poems regarding fault-finding he stated that "O, happy the soul that saw its own fault, many of the fault you see in others, dear reader, are your own nature reflected in them, as the prophet said " the faithful are mirrors to one another." (Rumi, Masnavi-e Manavi, 13th Century). Fault-finding is based on the assumption that mental self is better than others and clear from any fault, but everybody else have some wrong doings. Thus, mental self is scanning the environment to find someone to blame for something he does not like or approve. Muhammad, the prophet of Islam once said, "Happy are those who find fault in themselves, instead of finding fault with others." (Koran,). Tussing identified a character type he called "Yes, but" which is a fault-finder. This person agrees with others, but always adds the unpleasant negative to their observations (Tussing, 1959, P. 316-323).

Dehumanization and Demonization

Dehumanization is a negative emotion committed by an individual mental self, group mental selves or government mental selves in order to justify the destruction of an individual, group or government mental selves that are considered as part of an outgroup. It involves a conscious process of de-legitimization and placing an outgroup into an extremely social category by labeling them with negative terms such as terrorist, revolutionary, evil, etc. to facilitate and justify their destruction. Dehumanization usually occurs when members of one group considers other members within the group as in-group with a pattern of hostility against the members of another group which they consider as outgroup. Thus, dehumanization is a process which the individual mental self or group mental selves use to justify and facilitate aggression and violence against a targeted group.

Grandiosity Cluster

Selfishness and Narcissism

One of the major characteristics of mental self is selfishness and narcissism in which a person does not care about other people but expect everybody else to pay attention and show carte and concern about him/her. A mental self with selfishness and narcissism expects everything to be revolves around him/her but he/she does not feel any responsibilities about other people. According to Fromm, "selfishness and self-love, far from being identical, are actually opposites. The selfish person does not love himself too much but too little; in fact he hate himself, … It is true that selfish persons are incapable of loving others, but they are not capable of loving themselves either." (Fromm, 1975, PP. 135,136). Mental self or ego is very selfish and ego- centric which is a form of selfishness or narcissism. The selfishness, narcissism and egocentrism all are associated with a sense of superiority or grandiosity.

Sense of Superiority

Mental self develops a sense of superiority and tries to show he/she is better, stronger than others while evidence demonstrates that this is clearly not true. Mental self considers self as special being and more important than others. This is also related to mental self, tendency to emphasize on duality of life and conflict between opposites such as good or bad always considering self as good and other people as bad. Mental self being an artificial and temporary transitory self is not able to expand self without having someone to compare with and someone to fight with. Comparing, conflict and fighting with other people helps the mental self to further develop an artificial sense of existence in the form of "I". Mental self not only tries to make his/her "I" more important than others, but also tries to go further and add material and non-material belongings to self and create a sense of existence as "I" and a sense of ownership as "My" wealth, money, house, luxury, position, status, role, power, prestige, privilege, etc. The bigger the "I" and the "My," the more sense of superiority or grandiosity is developed by mental self.

Adler (1927) suggested the concept of "Superiority complex," in which a person seeks superiority status over other people. The consequence of a sense of superiority is problem in the person's social relationship with others. People try to stay away from the person as much as possible. A concept related to narcissism, selfishness and egocentrism is a sense of self-aggrandizement or exaggerated sense of self-worth. Tussing (1959) proposed a character type called "I'm-the-best" as maladjustment. According to him, this person must constantly feel that he is outstanding. He strains to create an image of himself as the best. He exaggerates the importance of trivial accomplishments, avoid situations where he might be excelled, and gains status through bragging about himself and belittling others" (Tussing, 1959, 316-323).

Another concept related to selfishness is self- righteousness or a view of a person as a good person. Mental self, possesses an artificial sense of self-righteousness although evidence shows on the contrary that person has a major pattern of deviant conduct. Mental self has a tendency to self-exaggerate and loves grandiosity and superiority over other people. Mental self has also a tendency to be over–confident in many areas of life and in his judgement. Problem that arises from over-confidence is that the mental self may start several projects without paying attention to his limitations and consequently his projects fails.

Stress Cluster

Emotional Stress

Chronic stress is one of the major characteristics of mental self. Stress has been defined in many ways. It is a complex, dynamic process of interaction between a person and his or her life. It is an unpleasant state of emotional and physiological arousal that people experience in situations that they perceive as dangerous or threatening to their well-being. Stress results from failure to adequately cope with stressors. Another definition of stress is the "wear and tear" our bodies experience as we adjust to our environment. It has physical and emotional effects on us and can create positive or negative feelings. The positive effect of stress is that it motivates us to take action. It can provide us with new form of awareness and an exciting new perspective. As a negative factor, stress can lead to distrust, rejection, anger, aggression and depression. Stressors could be either internal or external. Internal stressors are associated with Physiological, biological, neurological, glandular and hormonal as well as cognitive, emotional, psychological, and developmental factors.

Physiological factors include physical disabilities and limitations; abnormalities in the sexual arousal and tension; unmet basic needs such as thirst, hunger, need to go to the bathroom, clothing, security needs, love, belongingness, acceptance, recognition, stimulation, cleanliness, and other basic physical needs; addiction; dietary restrictions; and heightened physiological arousal such as pain and physical discomfort, and other sensitivities. Biological stressors include genetic factors or chromosome abnormalities; hereditary factors; puberty; menstruation, and menopause in women, etc. Neurological stressors including neurotransmitters involved in the induction and enhancement of our negative emotions such as anger and aggression.

Organic Brain Syndrome, neurological damage or head injury; frontal lobe impairment leading to intermittent periods of irritability that escalate into an emotional response and diminished coping skills such as anger and impulsivity.

Hormonal factors could also cause different kinds of stress. Chemical imbalance in the brain is associated with variety of stresses. For example: a little or too much amount of hormones such as Testosterone, progesterone, beta-endorphin, nor-epinephrine, dopamine, epinephrine, and serotonin could cause emotional stress or distress. Medical and medication side effects could cause different forms of stresses. Psychiatric, psychological and emotional factors also are considered as main source of the stress.

Cognitive factors could also create a great deal of stress for human beings. Our thought,   perception, and attitude could cause stress for us. The way we think, will determine how we feel and, how we act? If we define our situation in a negative way, then we develop negative emotions and stress which may lead to inappropriate behavior. Communication factors are also important in causing stress. Inability to communicate our wishes, wants, and needs as well as our physical or emotional pain and discomfort can cause high degree of stress. Emotional factors could also lead to a high level of stress. Developmental factors are also major sources of stress.

External social and ecological/physical environmental factors are also considered a major source of stress. Stressors are largely a product of their environment. Thus it is important to identify the environmental sources of stress. Social environmental factors include overcrowding; high level of noise, direct or indirect provocation from others such as physical, sexual, and verbal abuse and threats; interruption in individual's daily routines; sudden transition or change in our daily life; major change in our job or work schedules; having a limited range of options; negative attitudes of others; negative situations or conditions; witnessing other people's misery, oppression and misfortune; competing with others in many areas of life; lack of emotional, and financial support; not being able to control our destiny or future; negative significant events in our life; conflict and power struggles; etc.

External physical environment such as lighting patterns; noise level from industries, factories, transportation vehicles, etc.; environmental temperature;

inadequate ventilation inside the buildings; air pollutions; exposure to environmental toxins and lack of space are also major sources of stress.

There are variety of non-medical and natural treatment techniques and strategies to deal with stress.

- Deactivate and stop our mental self from producing stress for us.
- Becoming aware of the sources of stress and trying to stay away from it.
- Recognizing what types of alternatives we have and what we can change.
- Reduce our mental self from impulsive emotional reaction to perceived stressful situation.
- Learn to moderate our physical reactions to stress.
- Redirect our mental self and keep ourselves in pleasurable and preferred activities.
- Engage in physical exercises that, produces hormones that energizes us and makes us joyful.
- Develop some mutually supportive network of friendship and social relationships.
- Engage in activities that are incompatible with stress such as yoga, thy-chi, relaxation exercises, deep breathing, tense-relax muscle exercises etc.
- Participate in recreation activities that are alternative, adaptive and replacement for stressors.
- Journaling or talking about our stress to someone and releasing our internal tension appropriately.

Childhood Emotional Problems

The emotional disorders of children are primarily a product of their childhood traumatic events, family dysfunctions and other negative social stressors and life experiences. The history of reinforcements (rewards and punishment), attachments and bonding, approval or rejection, pattern of interaction between the child and parents or caregivers, and developmental stages also play a major role in the development of children's emotional disorders. In addition to the parents and significant others, other network of social relationships such as friendships with peers, teachers, and neighbors are of major importance in the development of children's emotional disorder. The emotional disorders of children are classified into two major categories: (1) Internalizing disorders or psychoneuroses, and (2) Externalizing disorders or conduct disorders.

Hysterical symptoms, as described by Kessler (1966), typically take one of several forms: "(1) sudden emotional outbursts; (2) disturbances in sensation and movement; (3) alterations in consciousness, as in somnambulism, fainting, or multiple personality; and (4) temporary losses of the sense of reality, as in hallucinations which are experienced with some insight into their unrealistic nature." (Rie & Rie, 1980, p. 493). The behavioral symptoms of obsessive-compulsive disorder in children are repeated checking, repetitious worries and inquiries about the health of a family member. The behavioral symptoms of depression are: sad mood; low self-esteem; feelings of guilt; helplessness, hopelessness and worthlessness and lack of energy.

Abuse of children has a long history. It usually happens in three forms: 1 sexual abuse, 2) physical abuse, and 3) neglect and rejection of the child. Abused children consider themselves as a problem and may think that the reason for being abused is that something is wrong with them, thus developing feelings of low self-image. Some of these children try to punish themselves or their body by engaging in self-injurious, self-mutilation, and cutting themselves. One of many reasons they do engage in self-injury is to reduce anxiety. Self-injury is a self-preservation technique for many children who engage in it. The self-injury and self-mutilation relieves anxiety symptoms which could lead to psychosis or suicide if not released or reduced. Self-harm can have calming effect and helping them to have certain degree of control over their bodies and life. Of course this is a profound way of expressing emotions for a child. But they don't know better way of expressing their emotions in an appropriate way to keep it at mild or moderate way.

Temperament

Temperament is an aspect of personality that is concerned with the intensity, duration, frequency, and speed of emotional reaction. The term often is used to refer to the mood pattern of an individual. A person's temperament is a relatively stable mood pattern and shows that who the person really is underneath all that. A person may pretend to be what he is not to impress other people. However, his or her temperament makes him/her to develop certain emotion and behave accordingly. Based on the negative experiences of the past, traumas, abuse, or neglect, people may develop negative that may cause them to project an image of themselves that is not necessarily true to who they really are. These kinds of people will react to stressful situations by engaging in outburst of anger, verbal and physical abuse or by withdrawing from the situation to protect them. People with negative temperament usually have some unresolved issues and internal conflict that they never had a chance to resolve, thus they continue to suffer from experiencing feelings of anger, hurt, disappointment, fear, rejection, loneliness, grief, guilt, and/or shame. They build walls in their lives that leads to feelings of isolation, loneliness and lack of intimacy and friendship in all of their relationships.

There is considerable evidence that indicates the relationships between temperament and emotional and behavioral problems. Temperament is a hereditary trait. Thomas, et al (1968) was the first to study the relationship of temperament to the development of behavior problems in children followed from birth. They found that a "group of traits (high reactivity, predominantly negative mood, irregularity of biologic rhythms, and low adaptability) which were identified in the first few years of a child's life predicted the development of "active" behavior problems between the ages of 4 and 10." (Rie & Rie, 1980, p. 161).

III

Internalized Human Emotions

"Laughter tells of your lovingkindness, tears complain of your wrath; these two mutually contrary messages relate in this world about a single beloved. Lovingkindness beguiles a heedless man in such a way that he is not anxious about wrath, and commits sin; the other man wrath endows with hopelessness, so that he keeps complete despair. Love, like a pitting intercessor, comes to the protection of both these lost souls. We give thanks for this love, O God, which performs infinite lovingkindness; whatever shortcomings in our gratitude we may be guilty of, love suffices to make amends for it." (Rumi, 13th Century, 103) Translated by Arberry, 1968)

Internalized emotions are either positive or negative. Positive emotions produce some of the most wonderful experiences such as: Love, tranquility, a sense of empathy or sympathy, sense of caring, nurturing and affection, a sense of security, a sense of justice. Internalized emotions when occur with high intensity could become negative and destructive leading to abnormal behaviors such as personalization, greed or excessive desires and wants, envy or jealousy, guilt and shame, self-exaggeration or grandiosity, emotional reasoning, fear and anxiety, depression or sadness, self-abandonment, self-isolation, a sense of being rejected, frustration intolerance, and negative self-hurt and self-brainwashing.

Positive Emotions

Positive emotions come from our universal consciousness which is full of energy, light, creativity, joy and tranquility. Human strives for an emotionally meaningful existence. Emotional health or emotional well-being involves a balanced, stable, and positive affect; more positive emotions such as love and empathy, happiness, interest, and positive pride than negative emotions such as anger, fear, and anxiety; positive coping skills; and a high level of self-control, self-esteem, and self-regulation. One major aspect of emotional well-being is emotion regulation which is characterized by the ability to experience both positive or negative emotions without becoming overwhelmed by them and the ability to express those emotions moderately and in ways that are socially acceptable. "An optimal level of emotional tension is adaptive in helping the individual to solve problems and to overcome obstacles without any negative outcome for the organism…" (Rotenberg & Boucsein, 1993, p. 1). As Child (2001) put it, "Joyful thoughts can create joyful emotions, which in turn can create a healthy spirit that affects one's physical being".

Love as Emotion

Love is positive aspect of human life and it is a motivational factor which helps human to fulfil their physical, emotional and spiritual needs for intimacy and affection. Love radiates from the universal consciousness and penetrates all particles of the universe. In human, the rhythm of love is parallel to the rhythm of human heart. With every heart beat we are reminded that we are alive and we need to be one with the living life and with our beloved. Rumi the Persian poet, philosopher, and mystic of Thirteen century, emphasized on love as being the most important emotion for human being. He paid attention to the psychological, emotional and physiological aspects of love. His poems, philosophy and ideas concentrated on motivational power of love and its influence on human behavior. He believed that all the particles of the universe are held together by the love attraction and that the dynamic aspects of the universe and the movement of the planets, stars, suns, moons and all special germs are the dance of love and attraction. Erick Fromm (1956) influenced by Rumi also tried to show the power of love in two of his books entitled "Art of Loving," (1956) and "for the Love of Life" (1983). Peck (1983) in his book entitled "the Road Less Travelled," talks about a new psychology of love, traditional values and growth.

Love is a universal phenomenon and includes romantic love of human as the lover and consciousness or God as beloved, romantic love of a man and woman, love of family such as mother, father or children which are the extension of the love of consciousness. All the love stories in different cultures show the motivational power of love some times to the level that the lovers sacrifice themselves for the beloved. Decartes (1649) advanced one of the first psychological, theories of emotions, reducing the diversity of man's feeling life to six basic emotions such as "passion, joy, sadness, love, hate, wonder and desire." Darwin (1872) articulated one of the first scientific theories the emotions, arguing for the instinctive nature of the emotions, and demonstrated their biological utility in the perpetuation of the species. He believed that emotions are a unifying factor within human species.

While our thinking mind has a voluntary self-conscious evaluative quality, our emotional mind possesses an automatic and involuntary one. Problem with the mental self is that non-satiable desires of our mental self can be unleashed and create problem for us. The main solution is to resist the desires of mental self by redirecting ourselves to something more productive or positive. However, we also need to know that mental self is persistent and does not give up easily and we must not resist by opposing or suppressing it because it will manifest itself somewhere else, seeking gratification of its desires. We thus, have a better choice of distracting, diverting or redirecting our attention to a productive activity.

Love as a motivational force, continues and remain intense as long as the lover is separated from and constantly longing to unite the beloved. But as soon as the lover joins the beloved, the motivational power of love would not exist anymore because there would not be any need for it. Example of these love stories can be found in many cultures: The love story of "Lily and Majnoon" in Persian literature; "Romeo and Juliet" in British Literature ; "Joseph and Zuleika" in Egyptian culture; and "Anthony and Cleopatra" related to two cultures of Rome and Egypt in British literature show the motivational power of love and its influence on human behavior. The real love particularly the love of consciousness provides us with inner peace and harmony.

Rumi (13th Century) in his poems talks about a story of a girl who fell in love with a young man. She was separated from her lover and was taken to a king's castle in another city. She could not see her lover or any family member and gradually became depressed, refused to eat and lost weight, isolated herself from everybody, lost interest in everything and lost her beauty. Her basic need of love, acceptance and belongingness could not be met. However, after joining her fiancé and lover in a different city where they could spend some time together, she gained her physical, emotional and mental health back and she was not depressed anymore. In vein with Rumi, Maslow an American humanist psychologist also talked about human basic needs and considered love, acceptance, approval and a sense of belonging to a family or a group as one major level of basic needs in his offered hierarchy of basic needs. Maslow also believes that human should not be denied love and acceptance, because it creates diseases. He stated that "To summarize briefly, the loss of the basic need satisfactions of safety and protection, belongingness, love, respect, self-esteem, identity, and self-actualization produces illnesses and deficiency diseases." (1972, P. 22).

People use their perishable senses and buy perishable love. We should pass these two dry currents and instead be our own fresh stream. Our false friends holding our hands pulling us from one side to the other leading us to nowhere land. We should let them go off our hands and be our own leads. Instead of being amused with the reflection of our beloved in the dark, let take off the curtain and clearly see our real beloved. Let be in our own home town with our true beloved above the two worlds with good thought. Any time we are away from our source, we would have increasing troubles and sufferings. Our mental self also works under the rhythm of love but like any other negative emotional rhythm, mental self, engages in artificial love that is transitory and short lived, jumping from one artificial love to the next and never has a real commitment. Love rhythm for unstable mental self which works with duality of life and existence, is based on inner conflict. Mental self's love as an intense emotion can turn into the opposite intense emotion of hate at any moment. Thus the love rhythm is alternatively aligned with hate rhythm.

Spiritual beliefs have a significant influence on human behavior. Human religious beliefs are associated with their spiritual and higher human tendencies which themselves are based on the human conception of realities of this world. Spiritual orientation can provide human with love, internal peace, and tranquility and eliminates his/her anxieties and worries.

The experience of love is very complex. It involves intense feelings of ecstasy, despair, and uncertainty. Love relationships are central in people's lives. It is root of all emotions and disruption of it is a major cause of personal distress. Emotions such as happiness, joy, caring, trust, compassion, truth, contentment, satisfaction are all love-based emotions. The more involved emotionally and intensely two people love each other, the more there is a probability for emotional disturbance to be experienced by either or both parties involved if the relationship is disrupted. Because love and hate are two major and high intensity emotions and two sides of the same coin. The disruption of love relationship may lead to depression or suicide. Rumi, the Persian Poet, Philosopher, and astronomer, in one of his story poems, shows the depressing consequence of love when a girl is separated from her lover for a long time. He also explains the positive power of love to heal the girl when she is rejoined with her lover. Other examples are the story of Lilla and Majnoon and Shirin and Farhad (Ferdosi, the Persian poet), in Persian literature, Joseph and Zolaikha in Egyptian Literature, Romeo and Julliet and Anthony and Cleopathra (William Shakespier, the British poet and philosopher) in British Literature, and many other love stories that caused personal distress, disruption, depression, and even suicide. The love story of Shirin and Farhad also shows the motivating power of love and the distressing and destructive power of failure to join the lover when Farhad, a Persian Engineer, turns a hill into a castle as part of a pre-agreement contract with the Persian king to be able to complete the project so that he could join her lover, Shirin. He works for seven years to complete the project all by himself. However, both lovers commit suicide at the end when each is told that the other lover was dead.

People who are in love show some physical, emotional, and psychological signs or cues that are considered as indicators of love and interest in each other. The physical aspect of interest is in the characteristics such as leaning toward each other, physical closeness and proximity as a sign of intimacy, and a deep eye contact or gaze by each person look more often and deeply in the other's eye. The emotional cues are the excitement, high level of energy, and joy of each lover during the social contact. The psychological cues are happiness, level of motivation, future orientation and planning. The strong form of being in love is passionate love. It is a state of intense absorption in another, arousal, and longing toward unification and oneness. An important component of love is activation or excitement. People who are in love have a tendency to intensify their emotions toward each other. A healthy love relationship is one that is stable and both parties involved have interdependency, mutual trust and respect for each other.

As a form of emotion, love can be classified into many categories: "(1) Love between parent and child, (2) Brotherly love, (3) Motherly love, (4) Erotic love, (5) Self-love and (6) Love of God." (Fromm, 1956, PP. 6-69) Other forms of love are: (7) Passionate love. (8) Humanitarian love (9) Family love, (10) Friendship love, (11) Romantic love, (12) Unconditional love, and (13) Spiritual love, or a higher power. According to Rumi, All forms of love are extension of our love toward our universal consciousness. Positive self-love not selfishness is the origin of other forms of love. A person can't develop other forms of love without positively loving himself or herself and then generalizing the self-love to other forms of love. A person who hates himself or herself only generalizes his or her hate toward others and everything. Thus to be able to love and be at peace with others, first, a person should be able to love himself or herself.

Sense of Empathy and Sympathy

Mental self does not develop a sense of empathy and sympathy as related to low emotional capacity or intelligence. When mental self does not have enough emotional vocabularies of low intensity emotions or excitements, and only uses emotional words that are associated with high intensity level of emotional arousal, then, there would be some explosive and exaggerated behavioral consequences. A mental self, with a deficient mental system that can't understand his/her own emotions and excitement, would not be able to understand other people's emotions. If mental self is not able to understand and express his/her emotion moderately, would engage in high intensity emotional expression which usually is aggressive and out of proportion. Problem arises for mental self who is not able to understand and express his/her emotions because, then, he/she would not be able to understand other people's emotions.

The main consequence of this lack of understanding others people's emotions is not being able to develop a sense of sympathy or empathy. Lack of empathy and sympathy also involves a lack of appreciation of harm and damage and the negative impact we have caused for other people. Lack of sympathy and empathy creates real problem between the mental self and others and negatively affects his/her social relationship with others. A mental self with lack of sympathy or empathy will become isolated when others try to leave and stay away from him/her. "Affective empathy, an ability to sense another person's feelings given knowledge of his or her position, has as its prerequisite, a form of cognitive empathy, the basic ability to imagine how the world may look from someone else's stance." (McGuire, 2000, P. 84).

Empathy is a major positive emotion in which we are able to put ourselves in other people's position and share and feel their pain and try to experience their emotional condition. To show empathy is to identify with another's feelings and to emotionally put ourselves in the place of another. One form of lack of empathy is what Samenow and Yokelson called "artificial sentimentality." According to them, most criminals are sentimental toward their mother, their children, helpless people or animal, however, on the other hand, they may brutalize them merely to show how tough they ate... They conceal their sentimentality" (Samenow & Yokelson, 1993, PP. 289-295).

Empathy is one of the major aspects of emotional intelligence. In order for someone to be able to show empathy for another, he or she must be able to appropriately identify and express his or her feelings. Only then he or she will be able to identify and understand another person's feelings. The emotion of empathy can be used to empathize with both good and bad fortune of other people. Of course it would be easier for us to empathize with people who are more emotionally expressive. Once we identified another person's feelings, then we can acknowledge their emotions. The behavioral consequence of the lack of empathy is that it causes many problems between the person who does not have a sense of empathy and other people negatively affecting his or her social relationships with others..

Empathy simply means to identify with another person's feelings. Thus we have to be aware of another person's feelings before we can empathize with them. Empathy is to emotionally put ourselves in the place of another person to feel what other person is going through. The ability to empathize is directly dependent on our ability to feel our own feelings and identify them. If we do not feel certain feeling, it will be difficult for us to understand how another person is feeling. In order for us to really understand other people's feeling, we have to actually experience it for ourselves. When we can't relate to other people is because we have not experienced, understood, or expressed many feelings of our own. It is easier to empathize with people who are emotionally expressive than those who are not able to express themselves.

Mental selves, who could not identify, understand and express their own emotions would not be able to understand other people's emotions. Psychopaths are good example of people who do not possesses a sense of empathy. These people are unable to feel the victim's pain and sufferings. Empathy is also related to compassion. Psychopathology, the incapacity to feel empathy or compassion of any sort is one of the most important emotional numbness or neutrality. The ability to identify and understand another person's feeling is critical to emotional normalization. Acknowledgment of another person's feelings is another step in empathizing with him or her. Sense of caring, nurturing and affection is part of our spiritual sense and relates to our consciousness and is special kind of empathy. In the external world of forms and roles we as forms become attached to our forms and roles as well as to other physical and mental forms and we see everything as forms. But our real essence is formlessness and we are connected to our formless consciousness.

Sense of Justice

Justice cluster include negative feelings that we develop when we feel injustice and unfairness. It include negative feelings such as accused; cheated; mistreated; falsely; guilt tripped; interrogated; judged; prejudged; discriminated against; labeled; lied about; lied to; misled; punished; accused; blamed; prosecuted; sentenced; singled-out; under-estimated; invalidated; and robbed. Justice cluster is an emotional response to an attack to the individual's integrity which may cause a major emotional arousal in the individual.

Emotional Security

Our emotional security is achieved and maintained when we are aware of our essence or consciousness and become united with it. Our mental system and mental self constantly distract us and tries to cover and hide our essence and instead to strengthen itself and to activated its artificial existence. Thus to have emotional security, we should be accompanied by our consciousness and to deactivate our sense of mental self. A negative sense of security is developed when mental self tries to think about the unknown future thus, develops a negative feelings of uncertainty and insecurity. It include negative feelings such as abused; afraid; attacked; frightened; intimidated; overprotected; scared; terrified; threatened; under-protected; unsafe; and violated. As human we have a choice to be happy and joyful while connected to our consciousness or to be emotionally sad or depressed while we are trapped within our mental system and letting our deviant mental self to take over our life even if it is only an artificial and transitory being.

Negative Emotions

Human tries to escape and avoid an emotionally painful and meaningless existence. Pathological or high intensity negative emotion is always harmful and should be controlled or prevented through appropriate channeling and releasing tensions. Pathological emotion usually leads to pathological anxiety when a person experiences maladaptive emotional tension. However, normal anxiety is developed when a person experiences adaptive emotional tension. According to Linehan's biosocial theory (1986), negative emotions contribute to chronic para-suicide in individuals with borderline personality disorder. According to him individuals engage in para-suicidal behaviors to relieve negative emotions such as anxiety, tension, and anger.

Negative feelings of guilt and shame, emotions usually come in clusters. Emotional clusters are secondary emotions that are composed of many primary emotions. For example, anger is a secondary emotion that is composed of primary emotions of being insulted; pressured; cheated, etc. Fear, confusion, sadness, happiness, resentment, depression are other example of secondary emotions. The most important negative emotion and emotional behaviors are: Personalization, greed and excessive desires and wants, envy and jealousy, emotional reasoning, fear and anxiety, depression and sadness, low self-esteem, frustration intolerance, feelings of self- hurt and self-injury, self-pity, resentment, oversensitivity, feelings of self-disrespect and self-disapproval, emotional avoidance and approval seeking.

Personalization

Personalization is one of the major forms of internalized emotion or excitement for mental self. Mental self, scans the environment to find something and take personally a random or neutral event or situation and viewing it as a negative or threatening to him/her. The event or situation may be completely irrelevant and not relating to the person at all, but, the person becomes co-identified with the event or situation and reacts to it by internalizing a negatively perceived event through personalization process. A mental self who internalizes the negatively perceived events or problem, evaluate self as the cause of negative external event for which he/she does not have any responsibility at all. The negative consequence of personalizing other people problems or even neutral situation is producing emotional, mental and psychological pains and sufferings. People who become addicted to personalizing other people problems develop social conflicts and problem with their relationships with other people. Other consequences are becoming angry, irritated, and depressed and blaming self for events that does not have anything to do with the person.

Greed and Excessive Desires and Wants

Greed is based on uncontrolled passion and desire which can't be satiated and thus leads to high intensity lust and greed. Greed is a high intensity form of envy that is based on irrational fear of hunger, poverty, and famines. It is because of this intense irrational fear that people will become obsessive in collecting and hoarding wealth in order to reduce or eliminate their irrational fear. However, greed is evil because the greedy person, will most likely disregard the moral and appropriate means of obtaining wealth and thus will engage in evil and criminal activities to satiate his or her artificial thirst for wealth. Greed is a feeling of never being satisfied. High intensity greed is a negative emotion that motivates abnormal, deviant and criminal behavior.

There is no satiation point for individual who is greedy. People, who are greedy, put too much emphasis and become over-dependent on money, luxury and material objects. "The more one has, the more one wants, since satisfactions received only stimulate instead of filling needs." (Durkheim, 1951, p. 248). Greed is directly associated with fear. It is out of fear of not surviving that people engage in greed particularly when they try to accumulate wealth, money, food, etc. Greed usually will lead to destruction. However, greed can also be considered an instinctive reaction for self-preservation and reproduction of species. Thus a low level of greed is part of animals and human instinct and assurance for their survival. Gathering natural resources, food and water will help people to have a piece of mind that they can survive and achieve the continuity of their species.

Envy and Jealousy

Envy and jealousy are negative emotions or excitements that relate to the comparing characteristic of mental self which has to have someone to compare with self, no matter what the content of comparison may be. Comparison usually relates to either quantity or quality of something someone else have that the person with pain producing mental self does not have or have a little of it. The item of comparison can be something tangible such as money, gold, silver, house, car, and luxuries or non-tangible artificial concepts such as positions, status, roles, privilege, power and prestige. Mental self being an artificial and non-real self, always is trying to collect and hoard as much material or non-material things as possible to add something to self and make self, look more important and distinguished as compared to others. A person with a rigid mental self, concentrating on comparing self with others either develop a sense of grandiosity when he/she has more than others and develops a sense of inferiority and worthlessness when he/she has less material or non-material wealth. Problem arises from the fact that the person with rigid mental self can't have more than others all the time which leads to envy or jealousy and a feeling of inferiority. This negative emotion affects the person's social relationship and people try to stay away from him/her.

Envy is simply a negative emotion based on fear and a form of distress felt by people when they think that they do not possess the good that others do or that others getting ahead in wealth, prestige, and power and they are not. Envy distorts and then consumes a person's view of life. It is a major destructive force in human relationships. Envious people experience displeasure at the success, happiness, or achievement of other people. Low self-esteem, incompetence, mental and physical laziness and dishonesty are basic causes of envy. To reduce envy a person need to become independent, self-sufficient, productive, and produce what he or she is envious about. This cluster includes negative feelings that we develop when we are jealous of other people. Envy is a complex, unreasonable, and irrational feeling, and is charged with high intensity negative emotional energy. Envy is an emotion experienced by one who intensely desires something possessed by another. (Wikipedia, the Free

Encyclopedia). Aristotle once said that "Envy is pain at the good fortune of others. (Aristotle, Rhetoric, BK II, Chapter 10). According to Kant, "Envy is a propensity to view the well-being of others with distress, even though it does not detract from one's own..." (Kant, the Metaphysics of Morals, 6:459). Envy cluster includes envious; jealous; antagonistic; greed, hostility, etc.

The major difference between envy and jealousy is that envy occurs in a dyadic group of two people where one person is distressed by the good fortune of another person. Whereas, jealousy, occurs in a triad group where the subject is jealous of the rival as related to the beloved. A jealous person is usually afraid of losing what he or she already has or that someone may be planning to take something of his or her away from him or her. Most religions prohibit engaging in jealousy, envy, competitiveness, and arrogance as major reason for conflicts and unhappiness. Buddha-ism rejects these emotions and recommends that we should treat everyone as equal. Buddha teaches love, the wish for everyone to be happy.

Comparing and Jealousy is a major characteristic of mental self. Western culture promotes Jealousy and competition particularly in the areas of social, economic, political and sports. In general eastern cultures competitions and jealousy are considered negative traits. A jealous mental self gets along with other people as long as he/she is better off or has more material wealth, money and luxuries or non-material power, prestige or privileges. However, as soon as mental self's material or non-material wealth or belongings becomes less than others, his/her jealousy starts and intensifies and the conflict begins.

Emotion of Guilt

Emotion of guilt is one of the major excitements mental self uses to create pain to identify and preserve self. Guilt is a feeling that we develop when we feel responsible for an action that we regret. It is directed toward oneself rather than toward others. Sometimes we may feel guilty for something that we are not responsible for. Guilt is usually related to our wrong doing. Both Guilt and shame can serve positive or negative function depending on how we debate with ourselves and what type of lessons we learn from them. If we use the guilt appropriately, it helps us not to violate other people's right. Guilt and shame are both serious emotions based on self-condemnation and feelings of remorse.

Guilt is attached to beliefs about what is moral or immoral, right and wrong. When we engage in an immoral behavior, we feel guilty over our behavior. Thus, guilt is a defense mechanism which helps us to maintain the moral standards of the society and religious values associated with them. Guilt may serve either positive or negative function. It can cause positive changes in the way people behave. Or it may cause people to lose their confidence in themselves and develop low self-image. Like, hate and shame, guilt also causes some negative consequences such as self-defeating and self-punishing behaviors such as self-injury, self-mutilation, withdrawal, isolation, and substance abuse problems.

Feeling of Shame

Mental self, engages in many different type of deviant and wrong behaviors and then, start feeling guilty and shameful for his/her behaviors. For example mental self may disrespect, falsely accuse someone of wrong doing or make negative remarks about someone who is not present, and then, start feeling guilty and becomes shameful. Sometimes a mental self may send another person to a guilt trip by reminding him/her of a wrong behavior he/she committed in the past as a means of controlling or punishing that person.

Shame is defined as" a painful feeling caused by a sense of guilt, shortcoming, impropriety, and disgrace." Shame is also defined as "a painful emotion caused by a strong sense of guilt, embarrassment, unworthiness, or disgrace, one that brings dishonor, disgrace, or condemnation." (Thesaurus Dictionary, 2004). Shame is an emotion of self-assessment, a reaction or response to some internal factor such as our conscience, appraisal of our own behavior and external factors such as our relationships with other people. Shame is usually related to our negative nature or personality. Thus it is a defense mechanism to help us to check out our personality traits and nature.

Shame is both a personal and social factor which is controlled by societal values and personal and religious values. Low intensity shame, shyness, and humility are all considered as socially desirable. "Shame occurs when one feels negatively evaluated by self or others." (Scheff, 1990). Shame cluster includes negative feelings that we develop when we are not assertive to say or do what we want to say or do. It includes negative feelings such as Bashful; ashamed; belittled; embarrassed; humiliated; shy; humility, and guilt. According to Beck, "shame, is a combination of personal guilt and embarrassment for it before others. When we feel ashamed, we feel bad particularly because of what others may think of us. We can also feel ashamed of someone else with whom we identify. Thus feeling ashamed is opposite of feeling proud." (Beck, 2004, p. 7).

One of the behavioral consequences of shame is development of low self-esteem and shyness. Shyness, doubt, caution, and lack of self-confidence are also behavioral consequences of fear. Modesty, false humility and shyness are within the shame cluster. Modesty "is a reluctance to reveal oneself to others either physically, emotionally, mentally, or spiritually. A modest person does not necessarily feel inferior or superior but rather private. Generally modesty is moderation and balance in social expression based on accepted inhibitions. With such feelings people attempt to maintain public decorum and agreed upon styles of behavior." (Beck, 2004, p. 9). Some researchers consider shame as hiding behavior (Scheff, 1990), a desire to hide (Davitz, 1969, p. 83), and a wish to conceal (Nathanson, 1987:184). A major consequence of shame is self-defeating and self-punishing behaviors such as self-injury and self- mutilation, withdrawal, isolation, and depression.

Emotional Confusion

Confusion is an emotional status in which individual loses their contact with reality and may not be conscious of the people, time, and location. Confusion is defined as the inability to think with our usual speed or clarity. This cluster includes negative feelings that we develop when we feel confused; ambiguous; lost; etc. Confusion may be related to a variety of internal psychological, neurological, and emotional factors such as anxiety, mania, psychosis, delirium, dementia, depression or combinations of the above factors. Other factors that could cause confusions are: Fluid and electrolyte disturbances; infections; drugs or medications; alcohol intoxication; low blood sugar; head trauma or head injury; brain tumor; concussion; sleep deprivation; seizures; nutritional deficiencies such as vitamin deficiency and malnutrition; fever; sudden drop in body temperature (hypothermia); low level of oxygen, hyper/hypoglycemia and hyper/hypothyroid. The elderly population has a higher probability of developing confusion due many age related problems such as stroke, Alzheimer's, and Binswanger's diseases. Confusion may be temporary or permanent depending on what is causing it. It may be developed suddenly or gradually. The behavioral and cognitive consequences of confusion includes altered level of consciousness, a decline in intellectual functioning, difficulty in attention and concentration, disorientation, difficulty in making decisions, difficulty in recognizing people or places, a disturbed mental state, embarrassment, shame, and anger and aggression.

Emotional Reasoning
Mental self uses emotional reasoning which is a combination of distorted thought and feeling based on distorted attitude and belief system which is part of a person's mental system. Mental self who engage in emotional reasoning assume that their negative emotions are based on the reality of the situations, but, in fact it is based on artificial pictures or reflections of reality not the reality itself. The problem arises when mental selves consider their distorted feelings as a base for evaluating different situations, thus, assumes that their negative emotions which are based on inaccurate information reflect the way the world really is and expect others to feel the same way. Emotional reasoning relates in employing our lower brain or limbic system which is a center of emotions instead of using our upper brain or neocortex which is center of our thought, logic and intelligence. Emotional reasoning is related to the shortcomings and deficiencies of our mental self. The solution is to use our consciousness and the upper brain and not to react to any situation.

Human Fear and Anxiety

Fear and anxiety is one of mental self's major characteristics and it relates to mental self's psychological time and living in the unknown future. Fear of unknown and uncertainties of the future include our fear of dying, fear of losing our wealth and money, fear of losing our health and physical beauty, fear of losing our reputation, social status, position, roles, power and prestige. If we really pay attention to these fears we realize soon that this type of fear comes out of being attached and co-identified with material and non-material belongings based on our artificial sense of ownership. Anxiety is a byproduct of fear and both fear and anxiety are interrelated. If we are afraid to lose something in the future, then we develop major anxiety over this type of thinking and feeling. A person who is becoming intensely attached to the worldly materials would always be in a constant fear of losing them.

Some people are so afraid of the uncertainties that they try to procrastinate their projects with the hope that they can do it later. This type of elusiveness relate to the fear of failure. Mental self becomes anxious due to his/her emphasize on the life of the unknown future. Mental self not being happy at present, rushes toward the future to experience the happiness, however, the only happiness relate to the life of this moment which is real. Future is only a mental concept and a psychological time which does not exist at the moment. Mental selves with excessive worries experience obsessions that are very persistent. Obsessions are thoughts that intrude repeatedly into our awareness and intervene in our daily affairs. When mental self constantly and continuously is worried about the unknown future and the upcoming events that are not here yet, usually experiences obsessions that are unwanted, persistent and hard to stop.

Fear cluster include negative feelings we develop when we are afraid of somebody, something, or our life in general. Fear is both an exaggerated conscious negative thoughts and unconscious thoughts or impulses. A mild amount of fear is natural or normal. However, when we experience a strong and intense irrational fear, that's when we are most likely to engage in a maladaptive, abnormal, or deviant behavior. Thus it is the strong, intense, and irrational fear that is pathological. Fear is another major root of negative emotions. It is an unpleasant feeling of perceived risk or danger, which can be real or not. Fear may serve a positive or negative function. It may serve a positive function when it is used as an evolutionary instinct for survival in perceiving and avoiding life-threatening or dangerous situations. The extreme and high intensity form of fear is terror. Fear always includes extreme dislike or hate of some fearful stimuli. It includes negative feelings such as horrified; victimized; afraid; hysterical; agonized; Fear usually relates to disapproval by others; rejection; failure; losing control; dying; losing our jobs; offending others; being alone; pain; fright; paranoia; horror, and uncertainty. Fear may range from low intensity such as being afraid or worried to a high intensity emotion such as being terrorized. Worry is a low intensity emotion which may be extended through time. The negative behavioral consequence of intense fear is that people will avoid and escape the fearful object, condition, situation, or event which could have a major negative influence on people's social relationships. It may also affect the individual's social, occupational life. Fear can be used to either motivate or unmotivated people and control other people's life. Fear of punishment is a major form of social control of human behavior. Fear like hate is the opposite of love.

Anxiety is a basic or primary emotion and in its normal state is functional for human survival. Anxiety cluster includes anxiety, worry, and neurosis. Anxiety in moderation is fundamental response to threats and is a part of an alarm system to alert us of upcoming dangers or threats. Threat initially arouses the sympathetic nervous system, causing the person feeling the threat or danger to go into a state of alert. This occurs through the secretion of adrenalin by the pituitary glands, which evokes intense feelings of fear or anger. The adrenalin rush mobilizes the threatened person for hyperactivity either in form of fight or flight. Anxiety only becomes a problem when it interferes with our general life functioning with prolonged symptoms and persistent distress. Anxiety has some psychological, behavioral, and physiological symptoms. Psychological symptoms associated with anxiety include excessive worry, hyper-sensitivity, and reduced concentration and attention.

Behavioral symptoms associated with anxiety include avoidance, immobility, and behavioral disorganization. Physiological symptoms of anxiety are increased heart rate, sweating, respiratory problems, and abdominal distress. Factors that are causing anxiety are numerous and divided into internal factors such as oversensitivity, hyper-responsiveness, low threshold for stress, lack of coping mechanisms, emotional insecurity or external factors such as accidents, violence, wars, rape, divorce, death of a loved ones, abandonment, or any threats or dangers within the environment. Sometimes medical problems can create anxiety. Medical problems that are associated with anxiety are hypoglycemia, drug reactions, respiratory problems (Asthma), hyperthyroid, etc.

As humans, we try to cope with stress and anxiety through certain defense mechanisms. These defense mechanisms, temporarily protects us from sensory overloads. Examples of defense mechanisms are repression, regression, suppression, rationalization, projection, sublimation, reaction formation, compensation, fantasy, magical thinking, etc. which helps us to avoid or escape anxiety-producing situations.

Depression Cluster

Depression and Sadness
Mental self's depression and sadness is a self-induced problem and it is created when mental self uses psychological time of the past that is only a mental construct and does not exist at present. Mental self tries to live in the past and becomes co-identified with the negatively perceived events or incidents of the past which are associated with different types of physical, emotional, mental or psychological pains. Mental self is addicted to pain and always looks for something to be sad about. Mental self also has a tendency to become bored easily and does not know how to amuse self positively and productively. One of the main tendencies of mental self is internalized emotion or excitement. Mental self is addicted to different forms of pain including physical, emotional, mental and psychological pain and suffering. Mental self's happiness

is very short lived and does not last long. Mental self is never satisfied and nothing really makes him/her, happy. Other negative feelings which are associated with depression are: Feelings of self-abandonment, self-isolation, and self-rejection. Mental self always feels lonely even when lives among a group of people because if mental self, internalizes and maintains the negative thinking, beliefs, and emotions, would always be depressed no matter if he/she is alone or part of a large group of people.

Depression cluster includes negative feelings that we develop when we are dysphoric and sad. It includes negative feelings such as irritated; agitated; agonized; anguished; anxious; melancholy; miserable; mortified; bored; broken; bruised; callous; numb; paralyzed; crushed; cursed; despair; doomed; scared; entrapped; sorrowful; grieving; wounded; drained; drained; empty; exhausted; hurt; hopeless; helpless; worthless; sad; lonely; and suicidal feelings. Depressive symptoms may include sadness, worries, stress, anxiety, Excessive feelings of isolation and being alone. Depression may present as withdrawn behavior, irritability, and aggression directed at caregiver trying to motivate the person. Depression also includes sorrow, disappointment, and sadness.

People with high intensity depression such as a person with a rigid mental self, full of emotional pains and suffering, becomes resentful, unassertive, and has a low frustration tolerance. People with high intensity of depression are low in emotional adjustment, sense of responsibility, and a sense of control. They feel highly isolated and rejected and these feelings contribute to their inability to form close relationships. A depressed person, have a low self-concept and considers self, dull and boring. However, using negative self-defeating thoughts and assumptions, he or she develops a sense of helplessness, hopelessness, and worthlessness which keep him or her avoiding other people.

Another reason for depressed persons to avoid other people is their high level of mistrust. They convince themselves that they hate others and their assumption is that people will take advantage of them. Then they develop the emotion of bitterness toward others which leads to avoiding social interaction or relationships. Negative life experiences and certain personality patterns along with emotional instability along with other factors such as low self-esteem, or extreme pessimism about the future can increase the chances of becoming depressed. Depression is always associated with shames. Major consequences of depression as a major negative emotion are: self-defeating, self-injurious, self-punishing behaviors such as self-mutilation, withdrawal, social isolation, social conflict, and suicide.

Emotional Self-Injury

Mental self with depressive tendencies and associated negative feelings and thought processes engages in self-injurious behaviors to hurt his/her body to eliminate physical numbness or self-alienation. Self- injurious behavior relieves intense feelings and anxiety and is a way to externalize emotional internal pain and is a way to change and eliminate emotional numbness. Menninger (1935) suggested that self-injury is an expression of displaced anger. Self-injurious behavior occurs in people with suicidality involved with depression.

Mental self has a negative and pessimistic view of the things and by engaging in personalization, tries to internalize pains and other people's problems. This process would lead to a sense of guilt, shame and self-blames which is also associated with an intense feeling and desire to hurt and punish self, because mental self feels that he/she deserve the punishment. Self-injurious feeling and behavior is a consequence of self-hate, low self-0image, low self-confidence, low self-esteem and low self-worth. Self-hurt also relates to other negative feelings of self-put down such as negative self-brainwashing, self-deception, self- blaming. Another form of artificial mental activity is called "self-fulfilling prophecy." by (Thomas, 1999) which is a special form of brain-washing and expectancy in which we may tend to perceive what we expect to perceive regarding a situation, event or condition.

Self-deception occurs when a mental self tries to escape the reality and engage in deceiving self about the nature of reality and to pretend that things are different than they actually are. Thus, engages in an artificial and distorted delusions or fantasy. Mental self has a tendency to engage in self-deception because the reality is too painful to comprehend or accept. Mental self, also engages in self-brainwashing to create an artificial situation to maintain its existence. We need to know that mental self itself is an artificial being with artificial thoughts, beliefs, and excitements.

Suicidal Emotions

Suicide has a biological as well as psychological basis. Biological basis of suicide, relates to neuro-chemical imbalances (alterations in serotonin neuro-transmission) in the brain. People with borderline personality disorder have a higher tendency for suicidal attempts and self-mutilation. Several investigators considered suicide and suicide attempts as escape or avoidance response or intentional efforts to escape distressing situations (Bancroft, et al, 1976; Hawton, et al, 1982).

Low Self-Esteem

Low self-esteem or low self-image are characteristic of mental self and are sense of being nothing. A person's self-esteem is not stable through time and is constantly changing based on the person's life situations. Low self-esteem usually is accompanied by worthlessness, hopelessness and a sense of inferiority. Opposite of low self-esteem is an exaggerated sense of superiority and grandiosity. Some people due to the pain addicting tendencies of their mental self, continue to feel a low self-esteem or unworthiness not related to their life situations. Low self-esteem is an artificial sense that mental self, experiences. Person with a sense of low self-esteem become fixated in anger stage of grieving process which is turned inward resulting in worthlessness and hopelessness. The negative consequence of this emotional state or negative excitement is despair, feeling of suicidal ideation, failure to endure adversity and harm to self or others.

Low self-esteem is one of the major characteristics of depression. It is the consequence of negative self-evaluation and mental self or ego development that comes from continuous receiving negative feedback from people around the person. Mental selves develop a sense of low self-esteem in two ways: one way is by engaging in negative self-evaluation of their selves and the other way is by negative evaluation performed by other people of mental self. Continuous negative feedback within a dysfunctional family and inconsistent parental discipline and punishment results in diminished self-worth for the individual recipient. Low self-esteem is also related to a mental self-inability to see self-0accomplishments and positive qualities within self, because it is used to see only negative aspects of things. A person with this type of mental self develops behavioral symptoms of withdrawal into self-isolation, engage in crying, being angry and refuse to participate in own self-activities and self-0carte and become dependent on others to take care of him/her.

Frustration Intolerance

Mental self, being artificial and hypersensitive, has a low level of tolerance for frustration and situation that is harsh and painful. This is due to the tendency of mental self to have obsession with immediate gratification and seeking short-range pleasures. Mental self, low frustration tolerance is also related to his/her impulse control problem and high level of reactivity. The main problem that emerges due to mental self- impulsivity and reactivity is that, all actions are spontaneous without any real analysis and evaluation of the situation which in turn leads to an inappropriate reaction. Another problem related to high impulsivity and lack of frustration tolerance is for mental self, using psychological time of the past or the future and does not have the patient to wait for anything and wants to obtain everything right away. Frustration intolerance is an emotional deficit that relates to our definition or redefinition of a situation. Thomas (1999) developed the concept of the "definition of the situation".

One of the major emotional problems is low frustration tolerance. Research shows that family background plays a major role in teaching low frustration tolerance to the children. Typically, people who are easily frustrated come from dysfunctional families that are disruptive, chaotic, and lack adequate emotional communications. Low frustration tolerance occurs when the person who is confronted with social stressors develops negative emotion which severely impairs the ability to hear, think, and speak appropriately. People with low frustration tolerance are usually explosive, easily frustrated, chronically inflexible, and explosive. This kind of people, have a limited capacity for flexibility and adaptability with a low threshold and tolerance for frustration. They usually have a rigid, black-and –white thinking pattern. People with low frustration tolerance have an exaggerated sensitivity to unpleasant feelings, impulsivity, excitement seeking and low tolerance for boredom, and deficient motivation to control their behavior. The major behavioral consequence of low frustration tolerance is not being able to solve the complex problems that come up in person's life.

Self-Pity

Self-pity is another characteristic of mental self which is based on the assumption that people abuse, humiliate, deceive, betray and are taking advantage of the mental self. A mental self with a sense of self-pity takes a victim stance and feels cheated and tricked by others even if he/she is the one who makes the mistake. It is one way of escaping from taking responsibility of accepting fault. The behavioral consequence of self-pity is development of a sense of being rejected, lack of trust and become totally guarded around others. A mental self with self-pity alienate self from others and blames others for his/her problems. This type of person always hopes someone else will come along and solve his/her personal problems.

The main consequence of this type of emotion is that mental self can't have a productive and positive relationship with other people. Self-pity is one form of attention seeking behavior for mental self which seeks people attention by complaining about imaginary health problems. Self-pity is an attention seeking emotion and behavior and also serves as an escape-avoidance response to avoid a harsh situation, condition or a difficult task. One form of self-pity is self-blaming which involves a mental self, blaming self for something he/she is not responsible for. A different form of self-pity is called self-labeling which involves identifying ourselves with some negative labels that shows us as being bad which in itself, is a form of self-brainwashing.

Resentment

Resentment is another characteristic of artificial mental self and is based on either a real emotional psychological pain or an imagined pain other people have created for mental self. Resentment is a negative excitement that relate to the psychological time of the past and related perceived injuries that mental self maintains by holding grudges and not letting go of the real or perceived injuries. The more a person with rigid mental self intensifies the injuries, the more sense of hate, vengefulness and dislikes will be developed by the person and then he/she uses that as a justification for different types of deviant or inappropriate behaviors.

Gradually when mental self, stores resentment and stuffs anger through the psychological time of the past, it will turn into a sudden episode of aggression or explosive behavior. Resentment is an internalized anger that is caused by reacting to the neutral event of the past and as a consequence, developing anger and hate against other people. Some people experience a sense of catastrophe and develop physical symptoms as symptoms of disease and abnormalities. Mental self's extreme vulnerability creates extreme resentment.

Over-Sensitivity

Oversensitivity is an emotional arousal which occurs anytime a mental self feels an exaggerated sense of sensitivity toward anything that is not in line with mental self's feeling pattern and expectations. Individuals with this type of mental self becomes agitated, irritated and react negatively and intensely to even a minor disagreement with their views. Tussing (1959) proposed a character type called the "touch-me easy-I am delicate." According to him "this character is one who is oversensitive. He must be handled carefully since he is on the alert to being hurt by others... His behavior brings him a great deal of attention since his acquaintances must always be concerned about his overly sensitive reaction." (Tussing, 1959, P. 316-323).

Feeling of Self-Disrespect and Disapproval

Mental self has a tendency to feel disrespected or disapproved by others. This is partially related to the mental self's sense of oversensitivity. Mental self, expect everyone to respect and approve his/her conducts even from people who may not like him/her. If mental self does not receive the imagined self-respect from others, he/she tries to obtain it through manipulation force or acting out process. Mental self does not like anybody except self but, expects other people have an unconditional love and respect toward him/her. Mental self usually set the conditions of love and respect but it is always unidirectional. This condition is harmful to other people and that is why a mental self always have problem in his/her social relationship. Mental self is very inconsiderate of other people and does not wish to treat them with love and respect.

A mental self with this type of characteristic is not capable of developing a sense of empathy, sympathy or intimacy toward other people. Mental self has the major need of being respected and loved but does not care if other people have similar needs that need to be met. The best thing for mental self is to bring the level of expectation down and not to expect that everyone should pay respect to him/her. Another major negative trait of mental self is seeking approval from other people to feel good about self. Mental self continuously tries to please people so that other people view him as a good person but, this is a pretentious behavior to impress others.

Feeling of Being Rejected

Rejection cluster include negative feelings that we develop when we are rejected by our loved ones, significant others, or peers. It includes feelings such as being alienated; abandoned; alone; brushed off; confused; disapproved off; discouraged; ignored; insignificant; invisible; left out; lonely; misunderstood; neglected; rejected; uncared about; unheard; unknown; unimportant; uninformed; unloved; unsupported; disrespected; disconnected; excluded; and unwanted. It is important to know that feeling rejected is based on thinking rejected which means when we engage in the thinking error of being rejected we develop the feeling of being rejected. Although, being rejected is a fact of life, it may remain a neutral event and may not do any harm to us until, we internalize, personalize, and hold grudges on it.

When we are telling ourselves that we have been rejected by others, then, we engage in perseverative thought process of personalization and do not let go of it, the cumulative effects of such experience can cause variety of problems in our lives. We may internalize and become sad and depressed or we may externalize and become angry. Sometimes we may feel rejected based on our high expectation of love, acceptance, and approval from other people. And when we do not receive type of love, acceptance, or approval we expect, we may feel sad and loose our self-esteem and confidence. The most difficult rejection to experience is rejection in love that is very intensive and which may lead to major depression, suicidal tendencies or attempt, and even homicides. Thus feeling rejected is a function of thinking that we are rejected.

Emotional Avoidance

Emotional avoidance is an emotional response to harsh and unpleasant events or situations and is one form of escape-avoidance response. Mental self being addicted to pain may like to have low intensity pain to be amused but when the intensity of the pain highly increases and it becomes non-tolerable, then mental self tries to escape from high intensity pain by engaging in varieties of coping mechanism such as avoidance, procrastination or elusiveness. Mental self has a hard time to deal with harsh situation or adversities and likes to obtain everything without working hard for it. But nothing can be obtained without hard work. Mental self gets easily bored particularly when types of activities are not pleasant to him/her. Thus, the artificial solution for mental self is escaping boredom.

The main consequence of avoidance is being nonproductive and not being able to achieve major goals in life. Emotional avoidance is based on lack of trust and negative feelings that we develop when we do not trust other people or when other people do not trust us. It includes negative feelings such as cynical; guarded; skeptical; suspicious; skeptical; distrusted; untrusting; avoidance;

betrayed; cheated; cheated on; pessimistic; and paranoid. It includes negative feelings that are developed when we do not feel confident about ourselves and our abilities. It includes negative feelings such as in-confident; unsure;

IV

Other Characteristics of Emotions

Emotional Intelligence or Emotional Competence

In 1920, E. L. Thorndike, an eminent psychologist proposed that one aspect of emotional intelligence, "social intelligence," the ability to understand others and "act wisely in human relations," was itself an aspect of a person's IQ. Howard Gardner, a psychologist, developed the concept of Personal intelligence and proposed two types: (1) Interpersonal intelligence, the ability to understand other people, what motivates them, how they work, and working with others, (2) Intrapersonal intelligence, a correlative ability, tuned inward. This is the key to self-knowledge, and access to one's own feelings and ability to discriminate among them and draw upon to guide behavior. Gardner did not pursue the details of the role of feeling in personal intelligence. Instead, he focused more on cognitions about feeling. Emotional functioning plays a major role in the social competence of the children. Low level of emotional competence is associated with difficulties in social relationships and behavioral problems. Sarason (1981) identified factors such as problem solving ability, perspective taking, and person perception as being essential to socially competent functioning. Foster and Ritchey (1979) and Anderson and Messick (1974), defined social competence as the ability to be effective in realization of social goals.

During 1990, Mayer and Salovey, were trying to develop a way of scientifically measuring the difference between people's ability in the area of emotions. They found that some people were better than others at identifying their feelings, identifying the feelings of others, and solving problems involving emotional issues. Salovey includes Gardner's personal intelligence in his basic definition of emotional intelligence, and expands these abilities into five domains: "(1) Knowing one's emotions, (2) managing emotions, (3) Monitoring oneself, (4) recognizing emotions in others, (and (5) handling relationships. "in our everyday life, we are generally unaware of interpreting our inner feelings, as we are unaware of the organization and interpretation that guides our perception of the outside world." (Baron & Byrne, 1984, P. 500).

During 1994, Daniel Goleman, decided to write a book about "emotional literacy." Being influenced by Mayer and Salovey, Goleman, published his book, "emotional intelligence." He provided information on the relationship between the brain and emotion as well as emotion and behavior. He defines emotional intelligence as "the abilities such as being able to motivate oneself and persist in the face of frustrations; to control impulse and delay gratification; to regulate one's mood and keep distress from swamping the ability to think; to emphasize and to hope." He adds each emotion offers a distinctive readiness to act. Goleman define emotional competencies as "a learned capability based on emotional intelligence that results in outstanding performance at work" Golman, 1998b).

Goleman believes that people who are low in emotional intelligence are neither able to identify or express their own emotions appropriately or moderately. Since they can't identify or express their own emotions, they will not be able to identify or understand other people's emotions. As a result these types of people will not develop a sense of empathy. According to him emotions are contagious. We transmit and catch moods from each other. Goleman distinguishes between rational mind, the mode of comprehension we are typically conscious of and the emotional mind, a system of knowing, impulsive and powerful, if sometimes illogical.

Goleman explains how intense feelings can create distortion in reasoning, the lack of awareness of feelings can also be destructive, especially in evaluating the decisions on which our destiny depends, what career to pursue, whether to stay in a secure job, whom to date or marry, etc. Emotional intelligence is ability to precisely identifying, expressing, and communicating our emotions. Emotional intelligence includes a clear knowledge and awareness of feeling words and vocabulary with which we identify and express our emotions. However, most people do not have an adequate knowledge of feeling vocabulary. Emotional intelligence not only include the knowledge of feeling words, but also a knowledge of intensity of feeling words and classification of feeling words under certain clusters. For example anger cluster itself is composed of many feeling words.

Emotions are constantly developed by human beings throughout the day. These emotions are developed consciously or unconsciously depending on what type of mood we are in and what is the nature of our situation or condition. Emotional competence is an ability to experience, identify and express any of the emotions appropriately and moderately so that other people can recognize and respond to them. To be able to express our emotions appropriately, our emotions should match the content of our emotions. We may experience either positive or negative emotions at any time depending on the situation we are in. Of course positive emotions are fun and easy to deal with. However, negative emotions, are more difficult and painful and requires a great deal of energy and self-control to deal with. Dealing with our negative emotions depends on our social skills, emotional competency, and emotional intelligence as well as our past experiences and the history of our social learning. Many of the emotions will bring up memories of the past negative events for us.

Affect

Affect is a biological motivating mechanism that involves a set of facial, glandular, and muscular responses. Although affect influences different areas of the body, people experience it primarily on the face. It is a primary aspect of emotion, perception, cognition, decision, drives, interpersonal needs and behavior. Affect may be positive, negative, or neutral or flat. Positive affect include enjoyment, excitement, and surprise. Negative affect include negative emotions of anger, fear, distress, shame, disgust, depression, etc. A flat affect is a state of emotion-less-ness and abnormality. Affect can be identified by observing the individual's facial expression, body movement or listening to their tone of voice. Affect can be either adaptive or maladaptive. McCullough and et al (2003) distinguished between adaptive and maladaptive affect based on the level of explosiveness, control, and types of relationships.

> "Adaptive affect is first consciously experienced within the body, then, outwardly expressed interpersonally in a cognitively guided, fully controlled way. Adaptive expression of feeling is not explosive. Adaptive expression brings relief, makes things better, and can make relationships closer. Maladaptive expression of feelings is interpersonally destructive, resulting in worse feelings between people-more distance, frustration, misunderstanding, loneliness and hopelessness."

Affect control theory proposes that individuals cognitively harmonize themselves to generate feelings appropriate to the situation. The Individuals, who react negatively to their own inappropriate definition of the situation, are not able to maintain appropriate feelings. Thus individual's emotion is based on the relationships between their experiences and their definitions of the situations.

Emotional Consciousness

Emotional consciousness means being aware of our emotions and others. It is a function of our emotional intelligence that comes from our universal consciousness. Universal consciousness within human physical and mental system is aware of all human traits, attitudes, thought, beliefs and excitements or emotions. Mental self is responsible for creating inappropriate and negative thoughts, beliefs and excitements that are the sources of our cognitive distortion and high intensity emotions. Emotional consciousness includes awareness of emotions in terms of their types and intensity level. Intensity level includes high, medium and low intensity of emotions. For example furious is a high level intensity, angry is a medium level intensity, and dissatisfied is a low level intensity emotion. Examples of emotional categories are sadness, anger, fear, confusion, happy, etc. It also includes the identification and expression of our emotions.

Emotional consciousness is associated with emotional intelligence. Emotional intelligence includes an ability to identify the right occasion to be emotionally transparent. Travel of forms occurs from one place to another and from one form to another on the land, but travel of formless soul and consciousness occurs in the realm of unity. Consciousness will be released from our physical and mental system as soon as our physical body and mental system ceased to exist. An analogy for this condition and process is wood on fire. As soon as wood start burning, the flame and light energy will be released from the wood and the wood itself turns into ashes and minerals. Instead of being confused by our mental distortions, emotional problems, physical pains and sufferings as well as, we should be high on the love of life and consciousness.

Evolution of consciousness in human form is occurs within our physical mental system and then becoming released from our physical and mental system to join the universal consciousness. Our mental self produces our mental self that is composed of our thoughts, believes, opinions, excitements and emotions. The mental physical consciousness finally becomes free of the mental system and joins the universal consciousness upon maturity. The following figure shows the path of evolution of consciousness within human body and mental system.

Physical/Mental Consciousness _____	Becomes United with
Become released and Free	Universal Consciousness
From the Mental System	within Realm of Unity
And Mental Self	
Child Mental System_____	Mental Self Composed of
	(Thoughts, Beliefs,
	Opinions, Emotions)
Mental Self _____ Real, Objective Self _____ Selflessness	

Figure.3 (Evolution of Self and Consciousness within Human body)

Emotional Transparency

Emotional transparency means expressing our true emotions without trying to hide our real emotions. Of course to be able to engage in emotional transparency, we should be aware of our true emotions. To express our true emotions has therapeutic effect on us. However, we may not be able to show our true emotions at all time depending on our self-interests. Mental selves, prefers not to show their true self by putting a mask on and pretend to be one other than their true selves. This can be achieved by playing roles, impressing others and seeking attention from other people by not showing their real intentions or emotions. In general, people are cautious to reveal their true emotions for the sake of security. But to be secretive and lying about our emotions create other negative feelings such as guilt, shame, dishonesty which is in contrast with our emotional health. Another negative side effect of lying about our emotions is that other people misunderstand us and then we feel miscommunicated and misunderstood.

Emotional Thinking and Objective Thinking

Emotional thinking may occur when we think based on our primary emotions, which usually leads to our secondary emotions. Emotional thinking produces negative secondary emotions. Under careful observation of our consciousness, mental self creates negative emotions which at the same time provide warnings that something is wrong. Thus negative emotions should not be repressed but understood and dealt with. Rumi suggests that the best way to deal with anything that we may perceive as bad or unpleasant, is that we should not show any impulsive or sudden reaction and instead, use patience, silence and acceptance.

We may react or respond to our emotions in two ways: (1) The inappropriate, irrational, erroneous way that represses emotions or acts based on emotions, and (2) The appropriate, rational, and correct way that identifies, analyzes and expresses emotions in a moderate way. We may also deal with emotions in two ways: (1) suppression, in which a person is conscious of emotions, but temporarily set aside for experiencing at a more appropriate time, and (2) repression, which is based on denial of an emotion permanently forcing it out of the conscious mind. This process is a distortion of reality and pushing our emotion to the subconscious mind which may surface later and cause more intense problem for us.

Emotions and Motivations

Emotions are closely related to motivation, because they have the potential to move us toward certain objective or goal and are underlying causes of behavior. "Emotion can energize, motivate, and guide adaptive functioning, but its capacity to do so depend on the diverse processes by which emotion is regulated." (Thompson, 1990, p. 394). Some theories propose that distress or stress impairs one's motivation or one's ability to use self-control. Self-control tends to deteriorate during periods of emotional instability and negative mood. Emotional distress prevents rational thought and thus undermines the capacity to effectively control oneself. It may impair the motivation to control oneself in the normal and an acceptable manner. All of our actions depend on our level of motivations. Any blockage of our motivations may lead to frustration, anger and aggression.

Emotional Sensitivity

According to Rumi emotional sensitivity is an emotional trait that is a natural tendency of our mental self and relates to the intensity of our feelings that may occur at the low, medium or high level. The higher the intensity of our emotions the more emotionally sensitive we become. If a mental self is tolerant of the situations or events the degree of emotional sensitivity would be moderate, and person feels extreme joy and becomes compassionate toward others. However, if mental self is excessively intolerance of social situations or events due to mental self's impulsive reactions to those situations, then the degree of emotional sensitivity would be high and the person will experience emotional pain and sufferings. Emotional sensitivity also relates to mental self's concept of self, such as self-image and self-esteem. The more positive an individual's self-image or self-esteem is, the higher the degree of emotional sensitivity. The emotion of low self-concept or self-image creates negative emotional sensitivity.

Emotional sensitivity is also associated with the degree of reactivity of mental self and the emotional intelligence. The lower the emotional intelligence of the person is, the higher the degree of emotional sensitivity and vice versa. Mental self with low emotional intelligence has high level of emotional sensitivity. In order to cope with negative or inappropriate emotional sensitivity, we should be able to identify our emotions correctly, identify the reason for our emotions, and express our emotions moderately. In order to express our emotion moderately, we should use emotional words that are associated with low intensity emotional words. The high intensity emotional words are associated with high intensity emotions such as hate, furious, terrorized, etc. Thus emotional sensitivity could be positive or negative depending on the nature and intensity of the emotion, our emotional intelligence and how we can express and deal with our emotions.

Emotional sensitivity is a condition of being receptive to other's nonverbal cues such as their facial expressions, their affects, or body movement. Similar to empathy, emotional sensitivity is to notice someone else's feelings and to feel like him or her. Emotional; sensitivity creates social bonds and maintains the social relationships. Lack of emotional sensitivity in the forms of ignoring another person's feelings or belittling, rejecting, or minimizing the intensity of their feelings can lead to the discontinuation of friendships or social relationships. Some people may possess emotional hypersensitivity which is very harmful to other people. Martens (2003) hypothesizes, that "emotional incapacities and/or shallow emotions may be the result of negative, painful experiences in the past… Emotional hypersensitivity might be linked with: a history of neglect, rejection and abuse; insult; changes which are forced or not under control of the psychopath; obstacles that prevent the psychopath to do what he or she wants to do; narcissistic injury; broken friendships or relationships." (Martens, 2003, p.1-9).

Emotional Intensity

Emotions with low intensity are normal and adaptive and help us to survive and escape or avoid a harmful or stressful situation. Those emotions and generally does not cause major problems. Adaptive emotional tension increases the psychobiological resistance. However, mental selves' extreme and high intensity emotions or pathological tension or stress are always harmful and could cause variety of psychological and behavioral problems. Maladaptive emotional tension decreases psychobiological resistance and makes us vulnerable to the harsh environmental situations. Love and passion are positive high intensity emotions and sympathy and compassion are positive low intensity emotions. On the other hand hate and rage are negative high intensity emotions and sadness and shame are negative low intensity emotions. Individuals with rigid mental selves who develop extreme and high intensity emotions such as hate, rage, and fear may engage in irrational and/or dangerous behaviors.

People who let their emotions escalate to high intensity level are not able to experience genuine emotions without becoming overwhelmed by them and thus, express genuine emotions in ways that are socially unacceptable and cause problem for themselves and others. Love and hate are two sides of the same coin and both are high intensity emotions. A high intensity positive emotion such as love can turn into a high negative emotion such as hate at any time if one of the lovers becomes disappointed or betrayed. Love stories of different cultures throughout the history are good examples of negative consequences of high intensity emotions. The story of Laily and Majnun; Joseph and Zulaikha; Aziz and Negar; and Taleb and Najma in Persian culture; the story of Romeo and Juliet and Anthony and Cleopatra by William Shakespeare related to Roman and Egyptian culture as well as British culture, and many others are examples of this forms of high intensity emotions.

Emotional intensity is based on the emotional words we use that could generate from very low to a very high intensity of emotions or excitements. We could use different scales from zero to ten or from zero to five or just use three levels and classify our emotions into low, medium and high intensity emotions. The same way that our thought process can affect our emotions, verbalized thought in the form of speech and words also affects our emotions and behaviors. That is why Rumi recommends that we should be calm, quiet and stop talking and instead try to listen to everybody and every sound within our environment that can teach us many things such as the sounds of birds, animals, nature, wind blowing through the trees and leaves, thunders, humans and other creatures. When we talk our mental system is activated and makes a constant sound like the sound of bees in our ears which distract us from the real living life. When we are listening to our own bee like voices, we would not be able to listen to others and understand what they try to communicate with us. Expression of emotions or excitements and the related intensity of the emotions may be related to the subjective feelings people experience

Emotional Responsibility and Adjustment

Emotional responsibility is simply implies being responsible for our emotions or feelings. Our emotions motivate us to make choices which lead to our actions and behavior. Mental self who is addicted to physical, emotional and mental pains has problem controlling emotions. Thus to be responsible for our lives and to take responsibility for our actions, means we must take responsibility for our emotions and emotional reasoning. Emotional responsibility also involve the identification and control of our motives such as our fears, anxieties, desires, values, beliefs, and thought processes, setting personal boundaries between our emotional needs and others, and validate our emotions and the emotions of others.

Generally all of our behaviors are motivated by our emotional needs and desires such as need for love, approval, wealth, happiness, success, acceptance, security, certainty, pleasure, power, control, growth, etc. The relative degree to which we are motivated and reinforced by each of our needs depends largely on how much of our needs are met? What our value systems are? What our beliefs are? What our thought Patterns are? And what our fears and anxieties are? By taking care of our emotions and mental and psychological health and engaging in the appropriate thinking, action, and behavior, we will be able to be happy and emotionally responsible.

To be emotionally responsible, we should be able to appropriately identify our feelings, accept and express our feelings, and to set personal boundaries. Setting personal boundaries is the first step to protect and take care of ourselves. In order for us to set personal boundaries, we have to be able to express our feelings or emotions assertively and moderately which shows we are confirming and accepting our own feelings. Only then, we can take responsibility for our emotions, and behaviors. Emotional honesty is an important aspect of emotional responsibility. It means we should say to the other person, exactly how we feel, what we expect from him or her, and what consequence we may use but we need to say it in a moderate way using low intensity emotions. However, we should make sure that our expectation and the consequences we may use are realistic. To be emotionally responsible, we need to develop our emotional intelligence.

The main steps and aspects of emotional intelligence is first to be able to identify our emotion in a correct way, second, we should understand our emotions and third we should be able to express our emotion appropriately and moderately. Fitz Maurice (2002) talks about six levels of emotional responsibility or maturity including: basic emotional responsibility, emotional honesty, emotional openness, emotional assertiveness, emotional maturity, emotional understanding, and emotional detachment. A component of emotional responsibility is emotion regulation

Emotional Needs

Emotional needs are positive feelings individuals should experience in order to be happy, satisfied, and be able to grow. Emotional needs are met when individuals achieve or fulfill the real basic needs, not the psychological needs of mental self that are mostly artificial needs such as being heard, noticed, and recognized, being admired and appreciated and being treated fairly and with dignity and re-spect. All human would like being free and independent and not to be controlled by others. It is normal to expect to be loved, accepted and approved of; to receive affection; to be needed, valued, and understood, but we should not be too co-de-pendent on others for their approval, attention and support. It is helpful to have a positive network of social relationships, family support and commitment and to belong to a family, but the main law is interdependency not co-dependency. Everyone enjoys being safe and have a happy life, financial, and job security, and to be protected but there is no guarantees that everyone can achieve it.

When mental self becomes too emotional and raise his/her level of ex-pectation to the point that could not be achieved, soon he/she becomes disappointed when it would not be achievable. The main problem arises when mental self with an un-satiable appetite wants everything and likes to add as much as possible of material and non-material belongings to self, but this trait only increases the excessive greed, wants and appetite. All humans share emotional needs, however, each differs in the intensity and types of the needs based on how much of their emotional needs have been met at any point in time. As Maslow (1943) presented in his hierarchy of basic needs fulfilling the emotional needs for security, love, approval, acceptance and belongingness are some of the basic needs that need to be met for individuals to experience a sense of happiness, tranquility, and self-actualization. Unmet emotional needs may lead to frustration and a variety of psychological and behavioral problems. Thus, it is ok to achieve real basic needs, but it is not right to create unnecessary artificial needs and expect to achieve those needs.

Emotional Trauma and Disturbance

Emotional trauma is a reactive response by mental self, beings associated with a severe precipitating event or stimuli or to a prolonged exposure to an emotionally, psychologically and or physically unhealthy environment. These precipitating events or stimuli are physical, emotional, and sexual assault and abuse, natural disaster, exposure to combat or war, being victim of violent crime, major plane or car accidents, etc. Emotional Trauma may lead to cognitive, emotional, physical, and behavioral abnormalities. The cognitive consequences of emotional trauma are memory problems, especially related to the trauma, difficulty in attention and concentration, difficulty in recalling or painfully remembering a particular experience time, or location related to the trauma, insomnia and problem in falling sleep at night, feeling distracted, and making decisions.

The emotional consequences of emotional trauma and emotional dysregulation are: Depressive symptoms such as mood swings, a negative sense of self or feelings of helplessness, hopelessness, worthlessness, powerlessness, problem planning for the future, and, dysphoric mood, loss of interests, social isolation and withdrawal, poor appetite, sleep disturbances, etc., anxiety, fearfulness, obsessive and compulsive behaviors, irritability, anger, resentment, emotional numbness, a sense of not being connected to or fitting in with others, self-defeating behaviors patterns, and self-mutilation and panic attacks. Physical symptoms of emotional trauma and emotional dysregulation includes: eating disturbances, sleep disturbances, sexual dysfunctions, low level of energy, chronic and unexplained pain. Emotional trauma may lead to emotional disturbance which may include depression, Post-traumatic stress disorder, panic disorder, and many other psychological problems. Regarding the causes of emotional disturbance, hereditary, brain disorder or dysfunction, diet, stress, dysfunctional family, and lack of coping skills have been suggested as possible associates of emotional disturbance.

The major behavioral symptoms in children with major emotional disturbance are: Hyperactivity, aggression, self-injurious behavior, withdrawal, immaturity, learning difficulties, distorted thinking, intrusive thoughts, flashbacks or nightmares, sudden floods of emotions or images related to the traumatic event, amnesia, avoidance of situations that resemble the initial event, detachment, depressive symptoms, guilt feelings, grief reactions, jumpiness, over-reaction, sudden unprovoked anger, general and excessive anxiety, bizarre motor acts, abnormal mood swings, insomnia, suicidal tendencies, and altered sense of time.

Emotional Numbness

Emotional numbness is a maladaptive coping mechanism specifically intended to protect the individuals who experienced emotional trauma from the extremely agonizing feelings that one may come to believe are powerful and strong enough to really hurt the individual. Emotional numbing as a maladaptive way of coping can become an adaptive pattern for the individual over time and can hinder or interrupt the emotional maturity. Major ways for a child to deal with emotional trauma is either emotional numbing or magical thinking. These are ways of temporarily setting aside the agonizing pain of emotional trauma. Emotional numbing accumulates a lot of anger that in the long run may lead to depression and borderline personality disorder. Grief is another source of emotional numbing. Traumatic experiences such as grief and other physical, emotional, and sexual abuses when left unresolved can result in chronic emotional and physical numbness. Emotional numbness leads to a diminished capacity to feel joy or sorrow.

Emotions, Physical Space and Behavior

Physical space plays a major role in people's emotions and behaviors. Each individual have a n ideal physical boundary or space which he or she is comfortable with. Invasion of that boundary or physical space can create negative emotional and behavioral consequences. "All people have a zone of personal space, but personal space differs greatly from culture to culture. He identified three major distance or space: (1) Personal space. (2) Intimate space. (3) Social space or public space." (Hall,1966). Emotional response to our immediate environment can be positive or negative depending on the characteristics of the environment. Both over-stimulation and under-stimulation can play a major role in the development of negative emotions and maladaptive behaviors in humans.

Over-stimulation usually leads to trauma and post- traumatic stress disorder and under-stimulation and neglect may lead to depression and lack of motivation. Both over stimulation or under-stimulation may lead to sensory disintegration and could have many negative psychological, emotional and social behavioral effects on the individuals. When a child experiences sensory deprivation during the formative periods of development, he or she may develop different types of emotional or psychological problems in the future. The following figure shows the relationship between different environments in terms of being relaxing or non-relaxing versus stimulating, overstimulating and under-stimulating environments.

Stimulating

Non-relaxing	Relaxing
A stimulating, non-relaxing environment makes us emotionally dis-regulated, tense and dis-comfortable	A stimulating, relaxing environment makes us emotionally regulated, happy, and creative.

Over-stimulating

Non-relaxing	Relaxing
An over-stimulating, non-relaxing environment makes us highly emotionally dis-regulated, irritable and angry.	An over-stimulating, relaxing environment makes us emotionally dis-regulated, dis comfortable and worried.

Under-stimulating

Non-relaxing	Relaxing
An under-stimulating, non-relaxing environment makes us highly depressed, and bored	An under-stimulating, relaxing, environment makes us emotionally dis-regulated, sad and unhappy

Figure.4. (Stimulation, over-stimulation and under-stimulation
Vs Relaxing and non-relaxing Environment)

The relationship between human and social physical environment is not asymmetrical, it is mutual. Environment influences different people differently based on the way they react or respond to their environment. People with strong and stable emotions show less reaction and more appropriate response to the environmental stimuli, thus environmental influences are at minimum level. However, people with weak and unstable emotions show more reaction than the correct response and they will be more negatively affected by their environmental stimuli. In a stimulating but non-relaxing environment, we become emotionally dysregulated, and feel, tense and dis-comfortable.

In a stimulating and relaxing environment, we become emotionally regulated and feel comfortable, calm and creative. An overstimulating, non-relaxing environment makes us highly emotionally dis-regulated, irritable and angry. Most explosive and aggressive behaviors occur in this type of environment. An overstimulating, but relaxing environment, a person with emotional stability may become emotionally dis-regulated, but with low intensity of discomfort and dissatisfaction. An under-stimulating but relaxed environment may make us emotionally dis-regulated, but we may have low intensity emotion of sadness or being unhappy. In an under-stimulated and non-relaxing environment, we feel highly emotionally dis-regulated and we may feel major depression and becoming highly exhausted and tired.

Perhaps the broadest view of personal space is that when it is occupied by another person, there is a strong emotional reaction (Ashton & Shaw, 1980). In general, then, very close distances tend to magnify emotional responses, and both positive and negative feelings become more intense when distance decreases (Schiffenbauer & Schiavo, 1976). According to Baron & Byrne, reaction to invasion depend on one's physiological arousal, and cognitions or interpretation of the situation. The processes of physiological arousal and interpretation of the situation leading to different emotional responses is shown in the following figure:

		Interpreted as unpleasant and rude	Anger, dislike and aggression against invader
Invasion of personal space	Physiological arousal	Interpreted as hostile and dangerous	Fear and flight away from invader
		Interpreted as friendly and positive	Pleasure and helpfulness to invader

Figure.6 Baron & Byrne (1984, P. 458).

"When another individual enters your personal space, the initial response seems to be on increase in your physiological arousal. Depending on your interpretation of the situation, you apply quite different labels to your aroused state. As a function of what label is applied, your actual response to an invasion can be as varied as aggression, escape, and helpfulness." (Baron & Byrne, 1984, P. 459).

The relationships between perception of aggression and personal space or distance, has long been established. When individual's emotional and behavioral problems are seen as possible symptoms of a poorly organized environment, reorganizing the environment may prevent those emotional or behavioral problems. The major physical aspect of the environment such as material objects and arrangement of these materials could have a major effect on individuals living or working in any given environment. An appropriately arranged physical environment can provide organization and structure which will maximize learning opportunities and effective performance for individuals within the environment. The physical characteristics that are not organized appropriately may cause a variety of behavior problems.

As humans we are almost always in contact with noisy physical or social environments. Modern industrial society creates all kinds of unwanted and disturbing noises. In general, there are three main types of noises in our environment: (1) Natural environmental noises. (2) Human made noises, and (3) Industrially produced noises. "The definition of noise is partly subjective. If you don't like a particular sound and don't want to hear it, it is noise to you. Technically noise is a sound composed of many frequencies that are not in harmonious relation to one another. Legally, noise pollution is defined in terms of loudness and the length of time it continues. (Baron & Byrne, 1984, P. 471). There are several studies that investigated the relationships between the noise level and human physical, emotional and behavioral problems. Some researchers found that, exposure to sustained noise causes blood pressure to rise (Cohen et al., 1981, Cohen, et al, 1979)), hearing to become impaired (Glass et al., 1969), and general health to decline (Cohen & Weinstein, 1981).

The negative effect of air pollution on human health and behavior is very obvious and has been a matter of concern to urban sociologists, cartographic specialists, and engineers for a long time. Increasingly, the air pollution has become a matter of widespread concern to all of us due to the physical, emotional and psychological dangers of polluted air. The results of many scientific investigations demonstrated that there are substances in the air we breathe that can be exceedingly dangerous and can even kill us. People with diseases such as asthma, emphysema, or other lung diseases are more vulnerable to the polluted air. Air pollution may cause aggression or minor depression depending on the intensity of the pollution.

It has long been known that climatic aspects of our environment can have stressful effects on human emotions and behavior. Heat particularly seems to cause deterioration in human relationships. Temperature of the environment includes the temperature of weather and water. Many of us react negatively to hot or too cold temperature of the weather or water. Human can't function adequately in the extreme weather conditions. One of the major problems relates to the heat is that our performance declines as temperature increases. Heat also makes us annoyed, angry, and aggressive. Heat and humidity have been causally linked to adult aggression and to misbehavior in children (Baron & Bell, 1975; Russell & Bernal, 1977). However, both heat and humidity influences human behavior indirectly by lowering tolerance to stresses and aggressive threats.

Stress is a highly personal response and depends on the person's mental self and his/her reactivity tendencies. However, in addition to the personal characteristics of mental self, several environmental situations may almost always causes similar response including post- traumatic stress disorders, for majority of individuals. Accidents and natural disasters or events such as earthquake, eruption of volcanoes, forest or building fires, as well as tornadoes, storms, floods, and lightening can create, devastating damages, and put people in great physical danger and the related emotional consequences. These natural disasters can result in widespread destructions and death which could cause an extremely stressful situation. These events may lead to different types of emotional, psychological and physical illnesses. For example one of the major psychological problems is the post- traumatic stress disorder which may create physical symptoms such as flashbacks, sweating, nightmares as well as emotional problems such as depression, fears, and anger. Our stresses intensify, when we are not able to cope or adapt to the stressful situations. "Stress is the failure of adaptability. It occurs when the environmental or internal demands exceeds the adaptive resources of an organism." (Lazarus & Launier, 1978).

Mental self becomes highly active in military personnel, who are in combat during the war, who must deal with several anxiety producing and stressful situation regularly. They have to deal with the constant fear of capture, death, and mutilation of themselves or their peers or friends. Combined with other factors such as physical exhaustion, loss of sleep, separation from family and home, and doubts and confusion related to killing another human being intensifies the stress and anxiety they already have during the war. Physical illness during the war adds to soldier's stress due to their vulnerability. Soldiers or refugees who have to live in a concentration camp under the unbearable and harsh conditions will have intensified and heightened stress and anxiety. Human behavior during a disaster is influenced by many factors, including unexpectedness, suddenness, intensity, and duration.

People who are not strong or don't have adequate resources or skills are more vulnerable than others in coping with the natural disasters. They may display what has been called disaster syndrome, a state of confusion in which victims may complain of several physical symptoms such as nausea, insomnia, restlessness, and "the shakes." They may wonder around aimlessly. Some of the symptoms and signs that have been identified by Sarason (1980) include: death anxiety and a death imprint, terrifying dreams, death guilt, psychological numbing, impaired social relationships, and search for meaning. People who have experienced concentration camp and survived developed certain psychological problems or symptoms.

Other types of major stressful situations relates to stages of our life and transitions and sudden changes in our life. These transitions include : birth of a child; transition from family home to the nursery, kindergarten, or elementary school; puberty with its biological and social complications; major educational transitions; transition to the work environment; marriage and family responsibilities; having children and child-rearing; moving to a new place of residence; children leaving home; and finally retirement. Human mental self likes to be stable and permanent, but being an artificial existence is afraid of any major change in his/her life.

Environmental toxins have significantly and gradually increased since industrial revolution began. Approximately more than thousands of neurotoxins have been produced as a result of pollutant producing industrialization. These neural toxins have a severe negative effect on the pregnant ladies and their fetuses. Chaotic and altered environment turns on the brain safety system and through neural tubes affects developmental processes. Environmental toxins produce different behavioral, physiological, and cognitive changes and abnormalities in an exposed individual. According to Ausubel (1988)

"… Unintentionally ingested poisons have made us violent and stupid… the industrial revolution… has poisoned many among us. "Lead and other metallic elements profoundly alter the nervous system, and thus intelligence, memory, visual retention, and dexterity." (Nriagu & Pacyna, 1988). "Bone lead levels in fact have been convincingly linked to delinquent behaviors." ((Needleman et al, 1996).

Recent research has shown that "the incidence of autism is higher where there is more toxicity" (Yazbak, 2004). For example, aluminum toxicity "can produce a number of clinical signs and symptoms. Common are excessive headaches, abnormal heart rhythm,   depression, numbness of the hands and feet and blurred vision" (Kilburn and Warshaw, 1993). Aluminum toxicity has been shown "to produce impairment in choice reaction time, long-term memory, psychomotor speed, and recall on affected individuals as compared to controls" (Wills and Savory, 1985). Other symptoms that has been identified through many studies include: behavioral difficulties ((Goyer 1991); Alzheimer's disease, Parkinson's disease, and dementia (Berkum 1986; Goyer 1991; Shore and Wyatt, 1983). "Chronic exposure to copper produces psychiatric disturbances, depression, suicidal tendencies and aggressive behavior." (Goyer, 1991a). Lead may cause behavioral and mental and physical symptoms such as "fatigue, irritability, information processing difficulties, memory problems, a reduction in sensory and motor reaction times, decision making impairment, and lapses in concentration" (Ehle and McKee, 1990).

Chronic inhalation of mercury is associated with "a reduction of sensory and motor nerve function, depression, visual and/or auditory hallucinations, muscular tremors, sleep disorders, alterations in autonomic function (heart rate, blood pressure, reflexes), impaired visual motor coordination, speech disorders, dementia, coma and death" (Clarkson 1989; Goyer 1991b; Fawyer et al. 1983; Piikivi and Hanninen 1989; and Ngim et al. 1992). Other symptoms of mercury consumption are: "cerebral palsy, amyotrophic lateral sclerosis, Parkinson's disease, psychosis, and chronic fatigue syndrome" (Adams et al., 1983; Dales 1972).

Urban sociologists have shown that violent crimes occur more in some urban areas than others. Masters (1997) has developed "the neuro-toxicity hypothesis" of violent crime. This hypothesis holds that, toxic pollutants such as leads and manganese causes learning disabilities, an increase in aggressive behavior, and loss of control over impulsive behavior. "Of course the pollutants, does not work independent from other social factors. Pollutants in combination with poverty, social stressors, alcohol and drug abuse, individual personality characters may lead to criminal behaviors. Pollution causes people to commit violent crimes—homicide, aggravated assault, sexual assault and robbery." (Masters and co-workers at Dartmouth College (1997).

Over-stimulating bright lights are very disturbing to majority of people. Intensive and bright lights are damaging to human eyes. These kinds of lights are more agitating and disturbing for people who are hypersensitive to light or have photophobia. Light can also affect self-stimulatory behaviors in autistic children.

Sound and music can have both, positive or negative effect on human psyche, emotions, and behaviors. It is well known that sound and music has a relaxing effect on humans. Several researchers found that music and sounds have a major influence on human psyche, emotions, and behavior. Certain sounds or music produces pleasant feelings and sensations and can positively influence our mood and affect (Grinde, 2000; Storr 1992; Deliege and Sloboda, 1997; North and Hargreaves,1997). Appropriate music in line with the human biological, psychological, emotional, and universal environmental rhythm, can create harmony and relaxing conditions. Music and sound travels through the air in a wave form. When music or sound hits human skin and ear drums it penetrate into the body and vibrates and stimulates every part of the body including the organs, tissues, glands, cells, molecules, atoms, neutrons, protons, electrons, quarks, etc. The vibration and stimulation of different parts of the body produces craving for movement. The human dance and movement is a natural response to music and sound. This is a universal phenomenon and we know that in every society or culture always dance and certain body movements are associated with music.

Sound and music also have a positive effect on human psyche, emotions, and behavior through the vibration and stimulation of human glands. When glands including the sexual glands are stimulated, they produce certain hormones such as adrenalin, beta-endorphin, encephalin, and serotonin. These are natural and positive hormones that make us joyful, happy, and naturally high. Miller (2000) considers the process of sexual selection as responsible for appreciation and evolution of music. Music particularly the sound of drums can also be relaxing to people due to a pre-history of reinforcement in the mother's womb. DeCasper and Sigafoos (1983) consider the musical rhythm of drums as relaxing sound due to its resemblance to the pulse of the mother's heart beat during the prenatal period which is also a sign of security and comfort.

However, Music and sound can also have negative effect on human psyche, emotions, and behaviors. Excessively high pitch sounds or noises are troublesome to many people. High levels of noises or sounds are more distractive and agitating to people with hearing hypersensitivity. Chronic contact with high pitch sounds decreases the human hearing ability in the long run. High level of noise can be distracting, decreasing the ability to concentrate or pay attention, and make people confused. For example, People with autism are very sensitive to sound and noise. Rumi (1200), a Persian poet considered the winning sound of flout as a sound of separation from our origin, source, or God, and mourning and yearning for rejoining to our origin. Pankstepp (1995) and Rendall et al., 2000) metaphorically, considered the music as a call of an infant crying for its mother. "Separation calls are expected to evoke powerful feelings in parents, and especially in mothers" (Pankstepp et al., 1988; Rendal et al., 2000).

Sound in the form of negative or aggressive words can lead to aggressive thoughts, perceptions, emotions, and behavior. Emotionally and negatively charged word such as hate can lead to negative emotional and behavioral consequence (Ellis, 1962). Historically, singing aggressive songs or lyrics during the war or battles facilitates aggressive behavior even killing other human beings. When mental selves, become highly emotional and their logic and conscience is deactivated, they only act based on their emotional states without paying any attention to the consequence of their evil act.

A broad range of chemical compounds and substances with different types of smell exist within our ecological system. These substances provide us with some pleasant olfactory sensory stimulation which attracts us to those smells and some unpleasant and disturbing olfactory sensory stimulation which we try to escape from or avoid as much as possible. A sense of smell is helping us to become aware of our environment, make sense of it and to be in contact with our external reality or social ecological environment. We can evaluate the freshness or rottenness of our foods through the sense of smell. The sense of smell is a predictor and regulator of our life within our environment. Through this sense we know what kind of flowers are around us or what is happening within the environment. Any abnormality of our olfactory system negatively affects our adaptation to the environment.

Human body is made in a way that we have to be moving, exercising and using our body parts on a regular basis. To be physically, emotionally, and psychologically healthy we have to receive constant motion sensory stimulation. Physical exercise stimulates our glands in the body which in turn produces several hormones such as beta-endorphin, encephalin, adrenalin, and serotonin. Lack of motion sensory stimulation is associated with a variety of maladaptive physical, emotional, psychological, and behavioral; problems such as boredom, stereotypic and maladaptive behaviors, repetitive movements, hyperactivity, fidgeting, depressive symptoms as well as poor circulation of blood in the body. Motion sensory stimulation decreases and sometimes eliminates a variety of maladaptive behaviors. Research has shown that vigorous aerobic exercise reduced maladaptive and stereotypic behavior (Elliot et al. 1994).

Our senses including visual, auditory, olfactory (smell), tactile, taste, motion sensory stimulation, and body positioning plays a major role in our emotions and behaviors. Through these senses we communicate with the outside and inside world and make sense of external and internal reality. Any abnormalities in our sensory functions, affects our sensations and, creates sensory distortions which may lead to incorrect interpretation, misperception, or incorrect appraisal of the environmental conditions or situations. This condition causes the individuals to have difficulty perceiving the world correctly which in turn may lead to wrong decision making and exhibiting inappropriate behaviors.

Many researchers investigated the relationships between colors and human emotions and behavior. The findings suggest that environmental color plays a significant role in stress perception. Previous studies found that room color have specific effects on psychomotor activity and emotional states (Hamid, & Newport, 1989; Thompson, & Gerhardt, 1985: Pellegrini, et al, 1981; Naksian, 1964). Some of the findings showed that there was a correlation between red color and emotional and physical stimulation. Pink had an enhancing effect on individual's mood, while blue had a depressing effect (Hamid, & Newport, 1989). Goldstein's theory of color perception showed that red has stimulating effects on human behavior. He also found that specific effects of red color correlated with an aroused or excited mood state (Nakshian, 1964). Green color was associated with inhibitory effects. There is evidence that color sensitivity is affected in individuals with mood disorders (Barrick, et al, 2000).

Emotion as the Main Aspect of Evil and Evilness within Mental System

Evilness is a negative and destructive state of mind which develops in human being over time when human begin using the mental system and develops the mental self. According to Rumi (13th Century) when a child is born he or she is neither bad or evil or good or angel, however as soon as the child begins using his/her mental system and develops the mental self, he/she begins to see the world and experience the world through his/her limited mental system that is limited by language and by the psychological time of the past and present. It is through the process of socialization and internalization of negativity, oppression, abuse, exploitation and many other negative life experiences that a child first develops negative thinking and then negative emotions or the state of "evilness". Similar to Rumi, Fromm (1956) proposed the concept of "necrophilia" or necrophilic personality to reflect the identity of evil. The necrophilous person is the one who loves death and destruction, to destroy for the sake of destruction. Fromm considers the genesis of human evil as a developmental process.

Rumi considers human mental system as the "Hell" and the mental self as "Evil" and believes that mental self becomes evil through time when human thoughts, beliefs, opinions and excitements or emotions are developed. The more sophisticated the human mental self becomes the more evil it gets. Peck (1983) also talks about psychology of evil in his famous book entitled "People of the Lie". He spells out the essence of human evil. To him people who are evil, attacks other people instead of facing their own failure which is composed of cognitive distortions of fault finding and externalizing the blame. People of the lie as Peck explains, engage in evil act and work in the lives of other people around them in everyday life situations. As he states, "We are not created evil or forced to be evil, but we become evil slowly over time through a long series of choices." (Peck, 1983, p. 82). Peck considers laziness and narcissism as the root of all human evil. He asserts that "Lying is simultaneously one of the symptoms and one of the causes of evil, one of the blossoms and one of the roots." It is why his book is entitled people of the lie. (Peck, 1983, p. 218). He stated that "In fact, the only power that Satan has is through human belief in its lies." (Peck, 1983, p. 206).

In "The Road Less Traveled," Peck defined mental health as "an ongoing process of dedication to reality at all costs." (Peck, 1978, p. 51). He states: "the evil deny the suffering of their guilt-the painful awareness of their sin, inadequacy, and imperfection-by casting their pain onto others through projection and escape- goating." (Peck, 1983, p. 123). According to Peck the evil easily fit the broad category of personality disorder. "Autism is narcissism in its ultimate form. For the complete narcissist, others have no more psychological reality than a piece of furniture.." (Peck, 1983, p. 164).

Rumi believes that evil does not exist outside of human mind and thought. It is within the solitary mind of the individual that the battle between good and evil occurs. Thus it is up to the individual human being to decide if he or she wants to be evil or good. Carl Yung's archetype "the shadow'" is the dark side of the ego, and the center of evil. In vein with Rumi, Boeree (1997) stated, "Symbols of the shadow include the snake (as in the garden of Eden), the dragon, monsters, and demons. It often guards the entrance to a cave or a pool of water, which is the collective unconscious. Next time you dream about wrestling with the devil, it may only be yourself you are wrestling with." Group evil is reflection of the individual's evil. "The effort to prevent group evil-including war-must therefore be directed toward the individual. It is, of course, a process of education." (Peck, 1983, .p.252). Human has a tendency to be good and behave positively when their basic needs are met, when pleased and receives pleasure, when comforted, confirmed, respected, accepted, approved, and loved, and has a tendency to be bad or evil and behave aggressively and violently when their basic needs are not met, when they are frustrated, suffering, revengeful, greedy, envious, jealous, oppressed, humiliated, neglected, abused, rejected, hated, threatened, not trusted, etc.

The Islamic view of Evilness and goodness is summarized by a Persian and Islamic scholar, Dr. Motahhari as follows:

> In the world there is good as well as evil, there is consistency as well as inconsistency. There exist abundance and scarcity both. There is light as well as darkness. There are progress and development as well as stillness and stagnation. But the existence of what is good, consistent, abundant, bright, and developing has the prime importance, whereas the existence of all that is evil, dark, inconsistent, and stagnant, is only subsidiary and secondary. Yet these subsidiary and secondary thing

play an important and basic role in the induction of what is good, consistent, harmonious and evolutionary. (Motahheri, 1997, p. 190).

Human Emotions, Sensations and Perceptions

Human sensation plays a major role in human emotions and behavior and it depends on our physical and social environment. It is through our senses that we make contact with our physical and social environment as well as our internal physical, neurological and emotional experiences such as physical pain and discomfort. We become partly aware of our physical, mental, emotional, psychological, and social self through our sensation devices. However, our relationship with our consciousness is through our spiritual senses.

According to popular beliefs, human has five major senses that include Visual, auditory (hearing), olfactory (sense of smell), a sense of taste and tactile (physical touch). However, there is another major sensation that most people are not familiar this is called "Kinesthesis" body's sense of movement in space. Yet another sense which is called "vestibular sense, provide information about body positioning and movement within the physical environment. I call this "motion sensory stimulation." Without active movement, we become alienated from our physical self and from our environment. When we sit in a place for an extended period of time, our body parts may go numb and we would not be able to feel our body part, thus we may become mentally confused and then, we become alienated from our own physical existence.

Human behavior is largely a function of individual perception. Human perception itself is an outcome of a combination of learned knowledge and information, the individual's environmental contingencies and the physiological, biological, and neurological make ups of the individual. Human behavior is based on both, the factual information or knowledge of the subjective or objective reality and delusion and distortion of the reality. The delusion or distortion as well as the factual awareness of the reality, is largely a function of human socialization and life experiences. The factual awareness of reality and appropriate appraisal of the facts may lead to appropriate behavior, while the distortion or delusion of the reality and inappropriate appraisal of the facts or situations may lead to deviant or maladaptive behavior. Thus human belief system which itself is under the influence of social, political and cultural institutions becomes the main means of controlling human behavior.

Sensation and perception are interrelated processes and work together to help us make sense of external reality. Before any mental processes such as organizing and interpreting to occur, first we experience the stimuli in the immediate environment. Individuals' perception of the reality is based on how they sense the reality based on the information they gather from the environment. If our perception of the reality is not based on the reality itself, we will experience an illusion. Illusions are being created in many areas such as magic, art, painting, music, lights, fashion designs, home designs, cosmetics, etc. All sensations are in response to a stimulus within the environment. Stimulus is any type of physical or chemical energy such as light, sound, heat, pressure, object, event, etc., to which we respond or react.

Our perception of the size of an object within the environment is based on comparing that object with other objects around it. If other objects are smaller in size than the object under our observation, the object will appear to be larger than when the objects around it are larger. Thus, an object's apparent or perceived size depends not just on the object itself, in isolation, but on the entire visual pattern or context of which it is a part. The Gestalt psychology, consider the pattern, context or form as a unit of perception. Modern theorists (Lindsay & Norman, 1977) considers perception as an active process which uses existing information received through sensory input to predict the future events. These theories emphasize that people actively interpret and try to make sense of sensory stimulation they receive through their senses.

Sensations play a major role in human behavior, and they are dependent on the environmental stimuli. It is through the senses that we make contact with the social and physical environment as well as our internal changes and states such as pain and physical discomforts. Through this type of contact we become aware of our physical, emotional, psychological, social, and spiritual self. "Through a process of transduction, the physical energy that the sense organs receive is converted into electrochemical energy for transmission to the brain." (Silverman, 1985, p.67). Disturbed sensory perception can cause many maladaptive behavioral responses including disorientation to time, place, person, or circumstances, inability to concentrate, visual and auditory distortions, inappropriate responses, talking and laughing to self, suspiciousness and hallucinations.

The lack of movement leads to numbness in our limbs and we lose our physical contact with our physical environment. This lack of contact with physical environment can lead to mental confusion and alienation from the environment. According to the information provided to us by physiological science, the sense of our limbs' position and movement's functions through receptors located in the muscles, joints, and tendons. An example of kinesthetic movement or active movement is walking. Another motion sense, the vestibular sense responds mainly to changes in the position or motion of the head. The vestibular sense is located in the inner ear. When we move, the fluids in the canals of our ears move and stimulate the receptors in the canals walls.

The main responsibility of the vestibular sense is to detect movement. It helps us to sense acceleration, deceleration, ascending or descending. The visual sense is the most important of our senses and it functions in reaction to the lights. Our eyes collect the reflected lights, focus the rays with its lenses, and cast a picture on its rear wall. Any discrepancy in our visual function can create false perception or illusions. The light is electromagnetic radiation or energy which is produced when electrons, negatively charged particles that circle atoms, bounce out of their usual orbit. Our mental perception of the size and shape of an object as well as its brightness remains relatively constant regardless of distance between us and the object.

When there is a discrepancy between what a person perceives and reality what we experience is an illusion. Our sense of hearing makes us aware of what is happening within our environment through the contact of sound waves with our ear drums. Sound waves enter the outer ear and our ear converts air pressure into physical vibrations. These vibrations create a neural impulse that is sent to the brain along the auditory nerve. Sound waves stimulate the sells within the body and body craves for movement. Dance could be considered a response to sound waves or music. The Sense of taste serves a number of important functions. It helps us to enjoy tasty food or drinks. It also discourages us from swallowing or ingesting potentially harmful substances. The taste receptors are located on the thousands of taste buds on the tongue. The receptors for smell are located high in the nasal cavity. Our sense of smell helps us to select the fresh and appropriate foods and to avoid the rotten foods. Tactile senses or skin senses contain many receptors scattered throughout the body which helps us to sense the pressure, pain, cold and warm.

V

Prevention and Intervention Strategies and Recommendation for Dealing with Negative Emotions or Excitements

"It is impossible to understand completely any human being or any single act of his behavior, just as it is impossible to understand completely why a particular wild rose bloomed under a particular hedge at a particular moment. A complete understanding in either case would imply an understanding of all cosmic process of their interrelations and sequences. But it is not harder to comprehend, the behavior of the "Unadjusted" or "delinquent" person, say the vagabond or the prostitute, than that of the normally adjusted person, say, the business man or the housewife. In either case we realize that certain influences have been at work throughout life and that these are partly inborn, representing the original nature of man, the so-called instincts, and partly the claims, appeals, rewards, and punishment-, of society,- the influence of his social environment. But if we attempt to determine why the call of the wild prevails in the one case and the call of home, regular work, and "duty" in the other, we do not have different problems but aspects of the same general problem. It is only as we understand behavior as a whole that we can appreciate the failure of certain individuals

to conform to the usual standards. And similarly, the unrest
and maladjustment of the girl can be treated only as speci-
fications of the general unrest and maladjustment. ." (W. I.
Thomas, 1923)

I have explained the emotions and excitements and emotionally induced behaviors of human beings in this book. Attention is given to the emotions and emotional determinants of human behavior and to the mutual interaction between cognitive and emotional factors. As the cognitive appraisal theories of emotions explains, we develop our feelings after appraisal and interpretation of events. Social contagion theory of emotions believes that emotions are contagious and we catch emotions from others. Rumi's ideas about the source of emotions states that we develop our feelings by reacting to our situation and then, we engage in secondary emotions that are either constructive or destructive depending on how we react or respond to different situations or events. The Cannon-Bard theory of emotion (1927) is based on the assumption that emotions lead to physiological changes within our bodies, while James Lang theory of emotion (1890) believes that physiological changes within our bodies lead to our emotions. Some believe that our thought process is causing our emotional arousal. There are other group of people who believe our mood and emotions biases our thinking and judgments. I believe that there is a mutual relationship between thinking and emotions. Both thinking and emotions affects each other.

Rumi Suggest the application of positive power of life and nature to prevent the exhibition of an intense and excessive emotion and excitement in human beings. To be connected to life force or consciousness will help us to be joyful and relaxed. As human we can be in contact with nature and different elements within the nature to maintain our equilibrium and balance in life. For example, water is one of the major elements of our life and nature and it is the main elements of our life and existence. Most part of our physical body is made of water and that connect us with water in different forms in the nature.

Water can be experienced in different shapes and forms in nature. Visual stimulation and experience of water in the form of clouds, fogs, snow, rain, hales, ice, vapor is also relaxing.

The humanistic approaches of Rumi focus on personal growth and interpersonal relationships and emphasize on the process of self-actualization, Transcendence, and mental factors within our mental system that prevents us from achieving it. Maslow is concerned with understanding individuals in terms of their distinctive human need to realize their own potential. Thus the primary purpose of human being is first to provide an appropriate environment in which individuals can develop a positive self-concept and become self-actualized and second for human being try to make their mental system quiet and simple and watch our mental system actions and reactions and prevent it from getting us into trouble.

The movement of water in the nature in many forms has therapeutic effect on human physical, mental, and emotional as well as psychological and spiritual dimensions. Observing water in motion creates positive and relaxing effect on our psychic dimension and helps us to develop positive feelings about ourselves and life in general. Listening to the natural sounds of water pouring from the waterfall down the edge and skirt of the waterfall; sounds of the waves of the lakes, seas, and oceans; sound of the water running through the river from the mountains toward the lakes, seas, and the ocean and hitting the cliffs on the way; sound of the rain falling down from the sky on the ground, provides human with a sense of relaxation, rejuvenation and joy.

Our interaction with water and connection through our sense of touch also is a wonderful experience. Swimming and floating in the water in swimming pool, lake, or sea is not only provide us with physical movement and exercise, but also helps us to relax. Washing ourselves with water is a positive and relaxing experience. Diving or jumping into the water from a cliff or from a position high above the water creates positive excitements in our life. The tactile relationship of human with water is feeling life to its maximum possibilities. Many people like to stay in the rain and let drops of water hit their body. Even animals and birds like to play with water. As we know today, two-third of our body is made of water and we could not survive without water. It is even more important than food for us to survive. Drinking water purifies our body from varieties of toxins that are collected within our physical system. It also helps us with our digestive system. When we get dehydrated, our body craves for water, because that craving is a signal for us that we should drink water to maintain our health and to guarantee our survival.

Wind is another natural phenomenon in nature that has therapeutic effect on human beings. Wind is the dance of the particles of the air within the space. When it touches and cresses our body, it provides a relaxing effect for us. Not only wind and air touching our body gives us a sense of relaxation but also the sound of the wind blowing through the valleys, forests or trees is relaxing and it brings the fragrances of flowers and natures to us which are also wonderful experience. Most of our musical instruments which we create beautiful music with them are using the movement of the air and wind through these instruments. Wind is also the vibration of the particles of the air within the space and similar vibration within the musical instruments produces beautiful music. Weaseling sound of music is also created by the wind while passing through the valleys and forests.

Physical movement also has therapeutic effect on human being. We could not feel normal without receiving constant "motion sensory stimulation," which normalizes our glands and productions of hormones within our body. Rumi believes that consciousness, energy and light within our physical system acts like a bird wishing to fly and hits our different body dimensions from all sides to fly freely into the sky and this is the main motivating power of our motions and dance. Movement and dance has therapeutic effect and provides us with relaxation and physical, mental, and psychological health.

Coping with Emotions

In order to prevent negative and destructive emotions, it is better not to be under the influence of negative news and information. Watching the negative news, listening to negative statements and reading about them in the newspapers or magazines are all continuous bombardment of our mental system with negativity and causes negative emotions. Part of the reason is the contagious nature of negative emotions and negatively producing emotions and excitement. Watching the news, listening to the news or reading about the news that are associated with people in misery, people getting killed or environment being destroyed would negatively affect human being who loves life, organization, beauty and relaxation. We should watch, hear, or read about positive, productive, and constructive news knowledge and information that could be beneficial to us and help us to relax and become more creative.

Another way to cope with emotions and excitements is that on the one side, we should not get too excited and happy when things goes well for us and on the other side, we should not get too angry and furious if something does not go according to our expectations. We should always be moderate. We should stay away from ideas, thoughts, beliefs, opinions, superstitions, and traditions that are artificial, false, temporary, rigid, and are associated with pain and sufferings. For example, we should not mourn and cry or become sad and hold grudges and suffer for a long time as related to a n event that we perceive as negative and painful. We should not concentrate on the old and negatively perceived events of the past or memories that are associated with negativities of the past that we can't change, because past is only a concept and does not have any real existence at present.

Another way to reduce or eliminate our negative emotions, excitements or thoughts is to live at the life of this moment and not to think about the unknown future which only causes us to develop negative and intense anxieties or worries. The news, thoughts, beliefs, opinions, language, speech which is loud thinking are not positive or negative in themselves, they become positive or negative for us when we try to define them as positive or negative. Thus, if we change our view of things, our glasses that we see through, and our interpretations and analysis of the events or situations then, everything would look different. Most of our thoughts, beliefs, opinions, excitements or emotions and traditions are recurrent perseverative phenomena and waste our time to engage in repetitive type of mental, emotional, and psychological activities which are non-productive and disturbing to us. Life constantly and repeatedly sends us messages from the realm of unity and tells us to become awaken and join us. We should use our spiritual eyes and move it around with coyness to see the consciousness and to make the evil eye of our mental self, blind.

We don't need to eliminated all our emotional, physical, and mental pains, because pains are awakening and gives us awareness that something fundamental is wrong within our physical, emotional and mental system. Thus we should eliminate the main source of pain not the secondary pain which is the result of something deeper within us. We should not jump and take medication or engage in the use of substances that makes us feel numb. Being numb and unaware of the pain does not really help us. Numbness is not real existence. Thus pains are wake up calls to become aware of real problems in our life and signs of major abnormalities within our different dimensions including physical, emotional, mental, psychological and spiritual dimensions. We should not maintain our negative emotions or excitements and carry them with us toward the unknown and non-existing future, because those negative emotions that we carry with us to different places and toward the future are our life that has not been lived. Thus we should live and use our life to the maximum level possible. The saved life is life that has been wasted and not used.

Rumi (13ᵗʰ Century) believes that human as consciousness is stranger in this world of forms including in human physical form, because instead of being in the realm of unity, it has become imprisoned in the realm of forms. Thus, formless consciousness is now trapped within all forms and the stability and continuity of the whole existence depends on it. We as human and as an extension of consciousness should constantly and continuously experience joy, beauty and tranquility which is the main traits of our source in the realm of unity. But within the mental system we have been separated from our source, the universal consciousness, we have been separated from other human beings and became alienated even from our real selves. Even-though our mental self is playing the musical note of separation from our consciousness, we have never been really separated from our source, because consciousness constantly working through us and leads us to the final destination that is becoming one with our source.

The happiness within this external world is artificial, transitory and temporary, but the joy and tranquility of our consciousness is eternal and limitless. We should constantly observe and be aware of our mental self and prevent it from engaging in resistance, fighting and having conflict with other people, instead, accept the events and situations as they occur without any judgement or reaction. Reaction only causes pain and causes conflict and problem. Our life that has been trapped within the mental system is the life that has been stolen from us and we did not have a chance to live it. When we are in any form of physical, emotional or mental pain and agony, our life that could be enjoyed will be stolen from us. Thus, life should be lived at this moment and not to be saved for the non-existing future.

A good way to reduce negative and destructive emotions is to eliminate our excessive needs for being recognized and approved by others. Expecting approval and recognition from others is an artificial sense of security and it is a psychological unnecessary and artificial need. The real sense of security comes from our within from our consciousness. Some people with a rigid mental self are searching for recognition and good name to make their mental self, look more distinguished and superior to others, however, this reputation seeking affairs are not real needs of human beings and in most cases causes major trouble for people. It is a major tendency of mental self to seek recognition, good name and reputation, to change its artificial and non-existence to something tangible, however, no matter how much tangible items or non-tangible items or belongings mental self, add to self, does not change the transitory and artificial nature of mental self. Thus the main solution is to be aware of our mental self's activities and prevent it from causing negative emotions for us or redirecting it to something more positive and constructive.

Lazarus (1993, 1999) and Lazarus and Folkman (1984) identified two major types of coping with negative emotions. "The first type or problem-focused coping strategy involves attempts to manage stressful situation by changing disturbing aspects of the environment to make it less stress-provoking. The emotion-focused coping strategy involves attempts to regulate negative emotions aroused within the stressful and disturbing environment." Similar distinctions made "between primary or efforts to modify a stressful situation and secondary coping strategies or efforts to adapt with the existing conditions. (Ebata and Moos, 1991).

Consciousness, Emotions and Human Behavior

Rumi's ideas about consciousness include two major forms of consciousness: One is the universal consciousness that resides within all forms and spaces in the universe and the other one is physical mental consciousness that is within our mental system. Any alteration or distortion in our physical mental consciousness can lead to psychological, emotional and behavioral problems. Consciousness-altering or psychoactive drugs, alcohol and other mind altering substances produce changes in our mood, thought, memory, attention, concentration, sense of time, perception, and other subjective experiences. Negative changes in any of these areas of functioning could lead to inappropriate behavior. Consciousness can also be altered through the process of meditation. Meditation includes a repetitive set of exercises or rituals to achieve an altered state of consciousness. These exercises may include chanting, repeating a sound over and over. Another technique of producing an altered state of consciousness is hypnosis in which an individual is susceptible to suggestions.

Consciousness in more limited utilization is simply defined as a state of aware-ness of ourselves, other people, places and times including the past, present and future. However, we need to be careful not to mistake the consciousness of real clock time with the artificial psychological time of the past or present which are mental constructs and do not have any relationship with objective reality. Thus, you not only have an awareness of your thoughts, but you also know what you are thinking. Our consciousness of the world affects the way we perceive the world, and our consciousness is in turn affected by our per-ception. However, consciousness is a dynamic process and changes constantly depending on our general emotional, psychological, and physical states.

Emotional and Behavioral Flexibility

Emotional and behavioral flexibility is an adaptive, flexible behavioral pattern that people use to cope with a dynamic, constantly-changing social and physi-cal environment. Society with many kinds of social, cultural, technological, population and ecological change necessitates adaptation and flexibility in relation to their emotions and behavior to cope with many stressful social, situational, and environmental events. To be emotionally and behaviorally flexible, we need to learn the required skills, knowledge and information and try to do an accurate appraisal of different situations instead of impulsively reacting to different events.

A rigid, black and white, static, and bipolar interpretation and analysis of a situation, will distort the picture of the reality we are dealing with which may lead to a distorted thinking, wrong emotions and wrong decision making and the related behavioral consequences. Emotional and behavioral flexibility also involves a comprehensive assessment of the facts before making any decision. Emotional and behavioral flexibility involves two major activities. (1) Try to change the environment if possible and (2) Try to use coping skills to deal with the unpleasant environment.

Emotional and behavioral rigidity is opposite of emotional and behavioral flexibility and it is a rigid and inflexible emotional and behavioral pattern that some people use to deal with the existing problems of daily life. Obsessive-compulsive, ritualistic, and stereotypic behaviors as well as fanaticism, hardheadedness, concrete thinking, black and white thinking, prejudice, and other biases and fallacies are some examples of emotional, cognitive and behavioral rigidity. Lack of knowledge, information and awareness of the environmental factors, rigid or concrete thinking, and high intensity emotional state are related to the negative behavioral consequences that may lead to inappropriate behaviors. To be more flexible and adequately respond to our environment adequately we need to do a comprehensive structural, motivational, and functional assessment of our thoughts, beliefs, attitudes, values, excitements and behaviors.

References

Adams, C. R., & et al. (1983) Mercury Intoxication Simulating Amyotrophic Lateral Sclerosis, JAMA, 250: 642-643.

Adams, G. L., et al. (1980) Environmental Influences on Self-stimulatory Behavior. American Journal of Mental Deficiency, 85: 171-175.

Adler, A. (1927) Practice and Theory of Individual Psychology, New York: Hartcourt, Brace and World.

Arberry, A. J. (1968) Mystical Poems of Rumi, The University of Chicago Press. Chicago. London. (Quatrains (I-200, 201-400).

Ashton, N. L., & M. E. Shaw (1980) Empirical Investigations of a re-conceptualized Personal Space, Bulletin of the Psychonomic Society, 15, 309-312.

Asubel, J. H. (1988) Technology and Society. 21, 217-231.

Ayer, A. J. (1946) Language, Truth and Logic, London. Victor Gollanz (2nd. Edition).

Bancroft, J. H. J. et al (1976) the Reason People Give for Taking Overdoses. British Journal of Psychiatry, 128: 538-548.

Barrick, C. B., & Tayler, D. J. (2000) Color Sensitivity and Mood Disorders: Biology or Metaphor? Journal of Affective Disorders, 67-71.

Baron, R. A., & D. Byrne (1984) Social Psychology: Understanding Human Interaction. Allyn and Bacon, Inc., Boston/London/Sydney/Toronto.

Baron, R. A., & P. A. Bell (1975) Aggression and Heat: Mediating Effects of Prior Provocation and Exposure to an Aggressive Model. Journal of Personality and Social Psychology, 31: 825-832.

Barrick, C. B., & et al. (2000) Color Sensitivity and Mood Disorders: Biology or Metaphor? Journal of Affective Disorders, 67-71.

Beck, A. T. (2004) A cognitive Model of Schizophrenia, Journal of Cognitive Psychiatry, 18: 281-288.

Beck, A. T. et al(2004) Cognitive Therapy of Personality Disorder (rev. edn). New York: Guilford Press.

Beck, A. T. (1976) Cognitive Therapy, Emotional Disorders, New York: International University Press

Beck, A. T. (1963) 'Thinking and Depression: 1. Idiosyncratic Content and Cognitive Distortions,' Archives of General Psychiatry, 9: 324-33.

Berkum, M. F. A. (1986) Aluminu : "A Role in Degenerative Disease Associated with Neurofibrillary Degeneration" Progress in Brain Research, 70,: 399-409.

Bernet, M. (1996) Emotional Intelligence: Components and Correlates, Paper presented at the 104th Annual Convention of the American Psychological Association. Toronto, Canada in a Symposium "Emotional Health and Emotional Intelligence" Monday, August,12, 1996. In http://www.somats.com/ei1996.htm.

Boeree, C. G. (1977) Personality Theories, Psychology Department, Shippensburg University.

Brad, P. (1934) the Emotional Expression after decortication with Some Remarks on Certain Theoretical View: Part I. Psychological Review. Vol. 4 (4), 309-329.

Bridges, K. M. B. (1932) Emotional Development in Early Infancy, Child Development, 3, 324-341.

Cannon, W. B. (1927) The James-Lang Theory of Emotions. A Critical Examination and an Alternative Theory, the American Journal of Psychology. 39, No. ¼: PP. 106-124.

Carver, C. S. & Scheier, M. F. (1990) Origins and Functions of Positive and Negative Affect: A Control-Process View. Psychological Review, Vol.(1): 19-35.

Cherrnis, C. (2000) Emotional Intelligence: What it is and why it Matters, Graduate School of Applied and Professional Psychology, Rutgers University. Piscataway, NJ. Paper presented at the Annual Meeting of the Society for Industrial and Organizational Psychology, New Orleans, LA.

Clarkson, T. W. (1989) Mercury. J. Am. Coll. Toxicol. 8: 1291-1295.

Cohen, L. E. & M. Felson (1979) Social Change and Crime Rate Trends: A Routine Activity Approach. American Sociological Review, Vol. 44: PP. 588-608.

Cohen, S. et al (1981) Aircraft Noise and Children Longitudinal and cross-sectional evidence on Adaptation to Noise and the Effectiveness of Noise Abatement, Journal of Personality and Social Psychology, 40, 331-345.

Cohen, S., & Weinstein, N. (1981) Non-auditory Effects of Noise on Behavior and Health. Journal of Social Issue, 37 (1):36-70.

Cooley, C.H. (1922) Human Nature and the Social Order, New York: Scribner's. In Scheff (2000) Shame and the Social Bond: A Sociological Theory. Sociological Theory, 18, PP. 84-89.

Dales, L. G. (1972) the Neurotoxicity of Alkyl Mercury Compounds. Am. J. of Med. 53: 219-232.

Darwin, C. (1872) the Expression of Emotion in Men and Animals, London: John Murray. In Scheff (2000) Shame and the Social Bond: A Sociological Theory, Sociological Theory. 18, PP. 84-89.

Davitz, J. R. (1969) the Language of Emotion, New York. Academic Press

Decasper, A. J., & Sigafoos, A. D. (1983) the Intrauterine heartbeat: A Potent reinforce for newborns. Infant Behavior and Development, 6, PP. 19-25.

Deliege, I., & Sloboda, J. (1997) Perception and Cognition of Music. East Sussex, UK: Psychology Press, Ltd. 461 Pages.

Descartes, R. (1649) In Passions of the Soul. Translated by Johnathan Bennett. (2010-2015).

Durkheim, E. (1951) Suicide: A Study in Sociological Method. Translated by: J. A. Spaulding and G. Simpson. New York: The Free Press.

Ebata, A., & Moos, R. (1991) Coping and Adjustment in Distressed and Healthy Adolescents, Journal of Applied Developmental Psychology, 12: 33-54.

Ehle, A. L., & McKee, D. C. (1990) Neuropsychological Effect of Lead in Occupationally Exposed Workers: A Critical Review. Crit. Rev. Toxicol. 20: 237-255.

Ekman, P. (2003) Sixteen Enjoyable Emotions, Emotion Researcher, 18, PP. 6-7.

Elias, N., and John Scotson. (1965) The Established and the Outsiders. London: Frank Cass. In Scheff (2000) Shame and the Social Bond: A Sociological Theory. Sociological Theory. 18, PP. 84-89.

Elliot, R. O., et al (1994) Vigorous, aerobic exercise versus General Motor Training Activities: Effects on Maladaptive and Stereotypic Behaviors of Adults with both Autism and Mental Retardation. Journal of Autism and Developmental Disorders, 24 (5), 565-576.

Ellis, R. A. (1994) Reason and Emotion in Psychotherapy, 2nd ed. New York: Birch Lane Publishing.

Ellis, R. A. (1994) How to Cope with a Fatal Illness: The Rational Management of Death and Dying. New York. Barricade Books, Inc.

Ellis, R. A. (1977) How to live with and without Anger, New York: Reader's Digest Press.

Ellis, R. A. (1962) Reason and Emotion in Psychotherapy, NJ: Lyle Stuart and Citadel Press. New York.

Fogarty, J. A. (2000) The Magical Thoughts of Grieving Children: Treating Children with Complicated Mourning and Advice for Parent. Baywood Publishing Company, Inc. Amityville, New York

Fawer, R. F., et al. (1983) Measurement of Hand Tremor Induced by Industrial Exposure to Metalic Mercury. Br. J. Industrial Med. 40: 204-208.

Fitz-Maurice, K. E. (2002) The Secret of Maturity: or How Not to be Codependent, Second Edition.

Fromm, E. (1983) For the Love of Life. Translated from the German by Robert and Rita Kimber, Edited by Hans J. Schultz, the Free Press, a Division of McMillan, Inc. New York, NY.

Fromm, E. (1956) Art of Loving, Harper & Row Publishers, Inc. New York NY.

Glass, D. C., et al. (1969) Psychic Cost of Adaptation to an Environmental Stressors, Journal of Personality and Social Psychology, 12: 200-210.

Goleman, D. (1998) Working with Emotional Intelligence. Bantum Boosk. New York. Toronto. London. Sydney. Auckland.

Goleman, D. (1995) Emotional Intelligence: Why it can Matter More than IQ? Bantum Books, New York, NY, USA.

Goyer, R. A. (1991) Toxic Effects of Metals, In Cassaret and Doul. Toxivity. The Basic Science of Poisons. Fourth Edition. M. O. Amdur, J. Doul, and C. D. Klaassen, Ed. Pergamon Press, PP. 662-663.

Goyer, R. A. (1991a) Toxic Effects of Metals, In M. O. Amdur, J. Doul, and C. D. Klaassen, Eds. Cassaret and Doull's. Toxivity. Fourth Edition. Pergamon Press, New York NY, PP. 653-655.

Goyer, R. A. (1991b) Toxic Effects of Metals, In M. O. Amdur, J. Doul, and C. D. Klaassen, Eds. Cassaret and Doull's. Toxivity. Fourth Edition. Pergamon Press, New York NY, PP. 623-680.

Grinde, B. (2000) A Biological Perspective on Musical Application, Nordic Journal of Music Therapy, 9, (2), PP. 18-27.

Hall, , E. T. (the Hidden Dimension, Double day and Company, Garden City, New York. NY.

Hamid, P. N., & A. G. Newport (1989) Effect of Color on Physical Strength and Mood in Children, Journal of Perceptual and Motor Skills, 69, 179-185.

Hawton, K., et al (1982) Motivational Aspects of Deliberate Self-Poisoning in Adolescents. British Journal of Psychiatry, 141: 268-291.

Izard, C. E., & et al. (1984) Emotions, Cognition, and Behavior, Cambridge: Cambridge University Press.

Izard, C. E. (1992) Basic Emotions, Relations among Emotions, and Emotion-Cognition Relations, Psychological Review. Vol. 99, 3, 561-565.

Izard, C. E. (1977) Human Emotions, New York, NY: Plenum Press.

Izard, C. E. (1971) The Face of Emotion. New York: Appleton-Century-Croft.

James, W. (1890) The Principles of Psychology. Vol.1, MacMillan. London.

James, W. (1890) Emotions, Williams & Wilkins Company, Baltimore, Vol. 1. (IX), PP. 188-205).

Kessler, J. W. (1966) Psychopathology of Childhood, Englewood Cliffs, NJ: Prentice Hall. In Rie, H. & Rie, L. (1980) Handbook of Minimal Brain Dysfunction: A Critical View, (Eds.) New York: Wiley.

Killburn, K. H., H. R. Warshaw (1993) Neurobehavioral Testing of Subjects exposed, residually to Ground Water Contaminated from an Aluminum

Die-casting Plant and Local Referents. Journal of Toxicological Environment, Health, 39: 483-4. Health, 39: 483-496.

Koestler, A. (1974) the Heel of Achilles: Essays. 1968-1973. London: Hutchinson.

Kolb, B. & B. Milner (1980) Observations on Spontaneous Facial Expression in Patients, In B. Kolb & I. Wisha (Eds.), Fundamentals of Human Neuropsychology. W. H. Freeman. San Francisco.

Kursman, C (1998) Liberal Islam. A Source Book, Oxford University Press, New York Oxford

Lang, C. G. (1922) Emotions, Harvard University, Vol. I. William & Wilkins Company. Baltimore.

Lazarus, R. S. (1999) Stress and Emotion. Springer Publishing Company, Inc. New York. NY.

Lazarus, R. S. (1993) From Psychological Stress to the Emotions: A History of Changing Outlooks. P. 18.

Lazarus, A. A. (1991) "Cognition and Motivation in Emotion," American Psychologist, 46: 362-67.

Lazarus, R. S., & Folkman, S. (1984) Stress, Appraisal, and Coping, New York: Springer.

Lazarus, R. (1968) "Emotions and Adaptation: Conceptual and Empirical Relations" In: Arnold W. J. (Ed.), Nebraska Symposium on Motivation, PP. 175-266. University of Nebraska Press, Lincoln, USA.

Lazarus, R. S., & R. Launier (1978) Stress-related Transactions between the Person and the Environment, In L. A. Pervin & M. Lewis (Eds.), Internal and External determinants of Behavior, New York: Plenum.

Lindsay, P. & D. Norman (1977) Human Information Processing, An Introduction to Psychology, 2nd Edition, New York. NY.

Lynd, H. M. (1961) On the Shame and the Search for Identity. New York: Science Editions. In Scheff (2000) Shame and the Social Bond: A Sociological Theory. Sociological Theory, 18, PP. 84-89.

Lyons, W. (1980) Emotion, Cambridge University Press, Cambridge, London. New York. New Rochelle. Melbourne Sydney.

Mark, J. (1982) "A Theory of Emotion," Philosophical Studies, 42: 227-242.

Martens, W. H. (2003) Emotional Capacities and Sensitivity Psychopaths, http:/goerzel.org/dynapsyc/2003/psychopaths.htm (PP. 1-9)

Maslow, A. H. (1972) The Farther Reaches of Human Nature. Viking Compass Edition, Viking Press Inc.

Maslow, A. H. (1943) A Theory of Human Motivation, Psychological Review, 50 (4): 370-96.

Masters, R. D., B. Hone & A. Doshi (1997) "Environmental Pollution, Neurotoxicity, and Criminal Violence," In J. Rose, editor, Environmental Toxicity, In Press. London. New York, Borden & Breach Publishers.

Mayer, J. D. & P. Salovy (1993) The Intelligence of Emotional Intelligence, Intelligence, 17 (4): 433-442.

McCllough, L., et al (2003) Treating Affect Phobia: A Manual for Short-Term Dynamic Psychotherapy, Part I, Theory, Evaluation, and Formulation, Guilford Publications.

McGuire, J. (2000) Cognitive-Behavioral Approaches: An Introduction to Theory and Research. University of Liverpool Publication, United Kingdom.

McKay, I. (2015) Social Justice Research, Vol. 138, No. 2. :PP. 1-268. In Michael P. Monitor Staff (2009) Vol. 40, No. 6: P. 34.

Mead, G. H. (1934) Mind, Self and Society, Chicago: U. of Chicago Press. In Scheff (2000) Shame and the Social Bond: A Sociological Theory, Sociological Theory. 18, PP. 84-89.

Miller, G. F. (2000) the Mating Mind. New York: Double Day and Company.

Motahari, M. (1977) Man and Universe, Ansariyan Publications. Qom. Iran.

Mowrer, O. H. (1960) Learning Theory and Behavior, New York. Wiley.

Nagim, C. H., et al. (1992) Chronic Neurobehavioral Effects of Elemental Mercury in Dentists. Br.J. Ind. Med. 49: 782-790.

Nakshian, J. S. 91964) the Effects of Red and Green Surroundings on Behavior, Journal of General Psychology, 70, 143-161.

Needleman, H. L., et al. (1996) Bone Le4ad Levels and Delinquent Behavior, Journal of the American Medical Association, PP. 363-369.

Neu, J. (2000) A Tear is an Intellectual Thing, The Meaning of Emotion. New York. Oxford. Oxford University Press.

North, A. C., & D. J. Hagrereaves 1997) the Social Psychology of Music, (Eds.) Oxford: Oxford University Press.

Novaco, R. (1977) A Stress Inoculation Approach to Anger Management in the Training of Law Enforcement Officers, American Journal of Community Psychology, 5, 327-346.

Novaco (1976) the Functions and Regulation of the Arousal of Anger, American Journal of Psychiatry, 133, P. 1124-1128.

Nriago, J. O. & Pacyna, J. M. (1988) Quantitative Assessment of Worldwide Contamination of Air, Water, and Soils by Trace Metals, Nature, 333, 134-139.

Oakley, J. (1992) Mortality and the Emotions, London: Routledge and Kegan Paul.

Ornstein, R. (1985) Psychology: the Study of Human Experience, Hartcourt Brace Jovanovich, Publishers. San Diego. New York. Chicago. Atlanta. Washington, D. C. London. Sydney.

Pankstepp, J. (1998a) Affective Neuroscience: the Foundations of Human and Animal Emotions. Oxford: Oxford University Press.

Pankstepp, J. (1998b) the quest for Long-term Health and Happiness: To Play or not to Play, that is the Question. Psychological Inquiry, 9, PP. 56-66.

Parsons, T., and E. Shills (1951) Toward a General Theory of Action. Cambridge: Harward U. Press. In Scheff (2000) Shame and the Social Bond: A Sociological Theory, Sociological Theory. 18, PP. 84-89.

Pellegrini, R. J., et al. (1981) Room Color and Aggression in Criminal Detention holding Cell: A Test of the "Tranquilizing pink" Hypothesis. Journal of Otho-molecular Psychiatry. 10, 174-181.

Piikivi, L., & H. Hanninen (1989) Subjective Symptoms and Psychological Performance of Chlorine-alkali Workers. Scand. J. Work Environ. Health. 15: 69-74.

Plutchick, R. (2001) the Nature of Emotions, American Scientist, Vol. 89, P. 349

Plutchick, R. (1980) Emotion. New York. Harper & Row.

Rendall, D., et al. (2000) Proximate Factors Mediating "contact" calls in Adult Female baboons Papiocynocephalus Ursinus) and their Infants. Journal of Comparative Psychology, 114, PP. 36-46.

Rie, H. & Rie, L. (1980) Handbook of Minimal Brain Dysfunction: A Critical View, (Eds.) New York: Wiley.

Rotenberg, V. & Boucsein, W. (1993) Adaptive versus Maladaptive Emotional Tension, Soc ml, and General Psychology Monograph. 119 (2): 207-232. In Http://rjiews.net/vrotenberg/adaptive versus.html.

Rumi, Jalalaldin Mohammad Molavi. (1278) Mathnawi-ye Manawi (Spiritual Couplets), a six Volume Poem, "Konia Manuscripts" Published five years after Rumi's Death (Persian Language)

_____. (1278) Diwan-e-Shams-e-Tabrizi (Diwan-e-Kabir) "Konia Manuscripts," Published five years after Rumi's Death in Persian Language, named in honor of Rumi's master Shams.

_____. (1278) Fihi Mafih Provides a record of seventy one talks and lectures given by Rumi on various occasion to his disciples, In Persian Language. English translation was first published by A. J. Arberry as Discourses of Rumi, New York: Samuel

Russell, M. B. & Bernal, M. E. (1977) Temporal and Climatic Variables, Journal of Applied Behavior Analysis, Vol. 10 (13): 399-405.

Safer, M. A., & H. Leventhal (1977) Ear Differences in Evaluating Emotional Tones of Voice and Verbal Content, Journal of Experimental Psychology, Human Perception and Performance, 3: 75-82.

Salovy, P. & J. D. Mayer (1990) Emotional Development and Emotional Intelligence, Basic Books. New York. Toronto.

Salovy, P. & Mayer, J. D. (1990) Emotional Intelligence, Imagination, Cognition and Personality, 9: 185-211.

Sarason, I. J. (1984) Stress, Anxiety and Cognitive Interference: Reaction to Tests. Journal of Personality and Social Psychology, Vol. 46(4): 929-938.

Schacter, S. & Jerome Singer (1962) "Cognitive Social and Physiological Determinants of Emotional Status." Psychological Review 69: 379-99.

Scheff, T, J. (2001) Commentary on "Shame and Community: Social Components in Depression". Personality, Shame, and Breakdown of Social Bonds: The Voice of Quantitative Depression Research. Psychiatry, 64 (3) PP. 228-239.

Scheff, T. J. (2000) Shame and the Social Bond: A Sociological Theory, Sociological Theory, 18, PP. 84-99.

Scheff, T. J. (1990) Microsociology. Chicago: U. of Chicago Press.

Schiffenbauer, A., R. S. Schiavo (1976) Physical Distance and Attraction: An Intensification Effect. Journal of Experimental Social Psychology, 12: 274-282.

Shore, D. & R. J. Wyatt (1983) Aluminum and Alzheimer's Disease, J. Nerv. Ment. Dis. 171: 553-558.

Silverman, R. E. (1985) Psychology. Prentice-Hall, Inc., Englewood Cliffs, New Jersey.

Simmel, G. (1904) Fashion, International Quarterly. X: PP. 130-55. Reprinted in the American Journal of Sociology, 62: PP. 541-559, In Scheff (2000)

Shame and the Social Bond: A Sociological Theory, Sociological Theory. 18, PP. 84-89.

Spinoza, B. (1677) Actions and Passions in (2001) Stanford Encyclopedia of Philosophy, Revised on 2013.

Spitzer, R. L., and P. T. Wilson (1975) "Nosology and the Official Psychiatric Nomenclature," In Alfred M. Freeman, Harold I. Kaplan, and Benjamin J. Sadock (eds.), Comprehensive Textbook of Psychiatry, Vol. 1 (2nd ed.), Williams and Wilkins, Baltimore (PP. 826-845).

Stevenson, C. L. (1963) Facts and Values, New Haven: Yale University Press: 210-214.

Stoessinger, J. G. (1985) Why Nations Go to War. Fourth Edition, New York, St. Martin's Press.

Storr, A. (1992) Music and the Mind, New York: Ballantine Books.

Thomas et al. (1968) In Rie, H. & Rie, L. (1980) Handbook of Minimal Brain Dysfunction: A Critical View, (Eds.) New York: Wiley.

Thomas, W. I. (1967, C. 1923) the Maladjusted Girl. with Cases and Standpoint for Behavior Analysis. Ed. Benjamin Nelson, Pref. Michael Parenti (New York: Harper Torch books,

Thompson, R. A. (1990) Emotion and Self-regulation. In Socioemotional Development: Nebraska Symposium on Motivation. Vol. 36, PP. 367-467. Lincoln: University of Nebraska Press.

Thomson, T. J., & D. L. Gerhardt (1985) the Limited Effects of Room Color on the Aggressive behavior of a Retarded person during Time-out Procedures. Tacoma, Washington: Biosocial Publications.

Tussing, L. (1959) Psychology for Better Living. John Wiley & Sons. PP.316-323. In Cox, F. (1973). Psychology (Eds.) WM.C. Brown Company Publishers. Dubuque, Iowa. P. 474.

Weiser, 1972. The translation of the second book by: Wheeler Thackston, Sign of the Unseen Putney, V T: Threshold Books, 1994.

Wikipedia, the Free Encyclopedia (2004) http://en.wikipedia.org/wiki.

Wills, M. R. & Savory, J. (1985) Water Content of Aluminum, Dialysis Dementia, and Osteomalacia. Env. Health. Persp. 63: 141-147.

Wood, S. E. &, E. G. Wood (2000) the Essential World of Psychology, Pearson Education Company Inc., New York, USA.

Wolpe, J. (1958) Psychotherapy by Reciprocal Inhibition. Stanford, CA: Stanford University Press.

Yazback, F. E. (2004) Autism seems to be Increasing Worldwide, if Not in London. BMJ. Letter 328: 226-227.

Yokelson, S. and S. E. Samenow (1993) the Criminal Personality. Volume I: A Profile for Change. Jason Aronson Inc. New Jersey. USA.

Zajonc, R. B. (1980) Feeling and Thinking: Preferences Need No Inferences. American Psychologist, 35 (2), 151-175.

www.ingramcontent.com/pod-product-compliance
Lightning Source LLC
Chambersburg PA
CBHW071403280526
45787CB00001B/412